PENGUIN  CLASSICS

POEMS OF HEAVEN AND HELL
FROM ANCIENT MESOPOTAMIA

ADVISORY EDITOR: BETTY RADICE

N. K. SANDARS studied, soon after the war, with Professor Gordon Childe at the Institute of Archaeology, University of London, and took the diploma of the Institute. She continued to work at Oxford, taking a B. Litt. degree in the prehistory of Europe, and therafter she worked on the prehistory of the Aegean, receiving a studentship a St Hugh's College, Oxford, a scholarship from Oxford University and a travelling prize from the University of Liverpool. She has travelled extensively in Europe and in the Near and Middle East, and has taken part in excavations in the British Isles and overseas. She has contributed articles to various journals and is the author of *Bronze Age Cultures in France* (1957), *Prehistoric Art in Europe* (Pelican History of Art, 1968), *Poems of Heaven and Hell from Ancient Mesopotamia* (Penguin Classics, 1971) and *The Sea Peoples* (1978). She has visited China and is at present at work on a book about the Silk Roads. N. K. Sandars is a fellow of the British Academy and of the Society of Antiquaries of London and a corresponding member of the German Archaeological Institute.

Poems of Heaven and Hell from Ancient Mesopotamia

TRANSLATED AND
INTRODUCED BY
N. K. SANDARS

PENGUIN BOOKS

PENGUIN BOOKS

Published by the Penguin Group
27 Wrights Lane, London w8 5TZ, England
Viking Penguin Inc., 40 West 23rd Street, New York, New York 10010, USA
Penguin Books Australia Ltd, Ringwood, Victoria, Australia
Penguin Books Canada Ltd, 2801 John Street, Markham, Ontario, Canada L3R 1B4
Penguin Books (NZ) Ltd, 182–190 Wairau Road, Auckland 10, New Zealand

Penguin Books Ltd, Registered Offices: Harmondsworth, Middlesex, England

These translations first published 1971

Made and Printed in Great Britain by
Cox & Wyman Ltd, Reading
Set in Bembo

To Nan (F.K.D.)

For so much

CONTENTS

Acknowledgements	9
Plan of Babylon	10
Introduction to The Babylonian Creation	11
The Babylonian Creation	73
Note on The Sumerian Underworld	113
The Sumerian Underworld	115
Introduction to Inanna's Journey to Hell	117
Inanna's Journey to Hell	135
Introduction to Adapa: the Man	167
Adapa: the Man	169
Note on A Prayer to the Gods of Night	173
A Prayer to the Gods of Night	175
Glossary of Names	177

ACKNOWLEDGEMENTS

I am most grateful to Professor G. L. Huxley, Mrs K. R. Maxwell-Hyslop and Miss Barbara Parker for advice on various points which has saved me from many errors; for those that remain they are not responsible. I am also grateful to Father Peter Levi s.j. for advice on matters of presentation and form. Them I thank particularly, but there are others, too many to name, whose suggestions and encouragement have made possible a rather daunting undertaking. To those who know the written sources it will be apparent how deeply I am indebted to the many scholarly works which are named in the Introduction and Notes to the various translations.

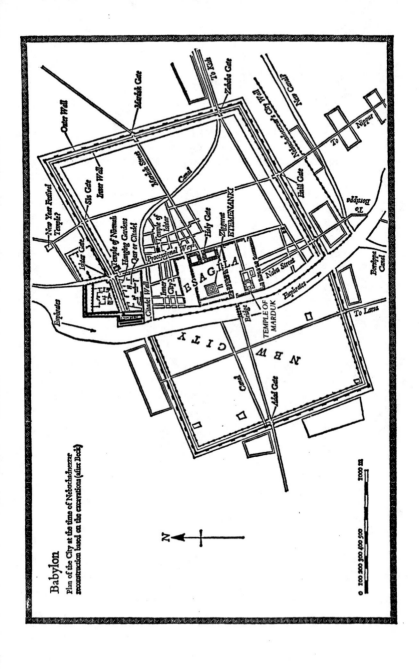

Babylon

Plan of the City at the time of Nebuchadnezzar
reconstruction based on the excavation (after Beck)

Introduction to *The Babylonian Creation*

I

Nimble and Light

The Creation is before all things a Babylonish poem. It is about the foundation of the world and the foundation of Babylon, the great city, the world's centre. Its hero is Babylon's own god, and it was sung or chanted by a priest of Babylon in front of the statue of that god. It is called *Enūma élish* from the first words of the Akkadian (semitic) text:[1]

> enūma élish lā nabū shamāmu
> sháplish ámmatum shúma lā zákrat

'When there was no heaven, no earth, no height, no depth, no name . . .'

What do we know of Babylon, and which Babylon do we want, for there are many? To most of us it came first in the nursery,

> How many miles to Babylon?
> Three score miles and ten.
> Can I get there by candlelight?
> Yes, and back again!
> If your heels are nimble and light,
> You may get there by candlelight,

and there we might go gliding through the dark between waking and sleep at the speed of light, of candlelight that is. Or is it the city of exile where the Israelites eat out their hearts beside

1. Long vowels, etc., are generally indicated on the first occurrence of a word in the text, and in the Glossary.

the Euphrates? From that present experience of fifty-odd years Hebrew poets and preachers turned Babylon into a huge metaphor: gaudy, sinister, beautiful and doomed. The invective and envy of Isaiah passed into the satire of Daniel, and the appalling judgement of the Apocalypse.

There is the Babylon described by Greek geographers and historians, ransacked by Xerxes and mourned by Alexander, who would have built it up again, but died there instead at thirty-five; and there is also the Babylon of the romantic imagination, fathered by St Augustine. There is ʿAmrān ʿAlī, al-Qāsr and Bābil, that cluster of little hills on the banks of the great river, crumbled brick, palm-scrub and dead water; and last there is the Babylon of the cuneiform writings, the 'happy home' of ancient gods.

Like the toys in the nursery cupboard they all come tumbling out of memory: Hammurabi and Cyrus, Nebuchadnezzar and Herodotus, Belshazzar's Feast and Alexander's death, Isaiah's taunt and Daniel in the lions' den, the Tower of Babel, 'Babylon the Great, the mother of harlots', and 'Babylon the glory of kingdoms, the beauty of the Chaldees . . .' The life of a metaphor can be longer and stronger than that of bricks and statues, and no other city, not even Byzantium, has lived on so indestructibly as a metaphor, after the reality of walls and palaces, of gold and blue glaze, was buried and gone. It was once so gone that, when Marco Polo crossed the Euphrates, *his* Babylon was a town in Egypt. But that medieval 'Babylon' was the heir of Alexandria, itself a Babylonish city, and the metaphor was remembered. The Great Whore of Revelation is the symbol of corruption and of retribution, whether it stands for Nineveh, for Jerusalem, for Rome or for Boston. If the Angel of the Apocalypse, crying 'Babylon is fallen, is fallen that great city', looks towards Rome, he only repeats Isaiah: 'And he answered and said "Babylon is fallen, is fallen, and all the graven images of her gods he hath broken into the ground."'

It is with these gods and their city that we have now to do, not with the end but with the beginning. In the fifth tablet of *The Babylonian Creation*, Marduk, over whose fallen image Isaiah exults, is the triumphant young hero shouting among the gods,

I have made Earth as the mirror of Heaven, I have consolidated the soil for the foundations and there I will build my city, my beloved home.

while some time very early in the sixth century B.C. Nabu-kudurri-uṣur II, or as we know him better, Nebuchadnezzar, King of Babylon, set up his boast in the street.

The streets of Babylon, the Procession Street of Nabu and Marduk my lords which Nabu-apal-uṣur, King of Babylon, the father who begot me, had made a road glistening with asphalt and burnt bricks ... Nabu and Marduk, when you traverse these streets in joy, may benefits for me rest upon your lips, life for distant days and well-being for the body ... may I attain eternal age.

This *via sacra*, a processional way of the gods, was the most magnificent street the world had seen. Herodotus probably knew it; he describes Babylon with much the same bemused admiration as Marco Polo expressed describing the cities of Cathay.

Such is its size, in magnificence there is no other city that approaches it. ... The houses are mostly three and four stories high, the streets all run in straight lines, not only those parallel to the river, but also the cross streets which lead down to the water-side ...

This straightness of the streets was true of Babylon centuries before; nor can it be altogether chance that the *streets* were remembered and left their imprint on the literature of the world, quite as much as Babel Tower (which may have been somewhere else). When Augustine appropriated them –

In that sixteenth year of my flesh ... I walked the streets of

Babylon and wallowed in the mire thereof as if in a bed of spices and precious ointments of Alexandria,

– already Babylon and Alexandria are linked; both alike attract and repel as high civilizations that are seen from outside and not understood. The appeal may be as unrepentantly nostalgic as George Russell's:

> Today was past and dead for me, for from today my feet
>   had run
> Through thrice a thousand years to walk the ways of ancient
>   Babylon
> The mystery and magnificence, the myriad beauty and the
>   sins . . .

or as sour and monitory as Robert Lowell's:

> Darkness has called to darkness, and disgrace
> Elbows about our windows in the planned
> Babel of Boston where our money talks . . .
>
> The flies, the flies, the flies of Babylon
> Buzz in my ear-drums while the devil's long
> Dirge of the people detonates the hour
> For floating cities where his golden tongue
> Enchants the masons of the Babel Tower . . .

When we have read *The Babylonian Creation* we know those masons, fallen gods working out the punishment of their rebellion.

> Alexandria's was a beacon tower, and Babylon's
> An image of the moving heavens, a log-book of
>   the sun's journey.

Yeats took the tower for his symbol, and the 'winding gyring spiring treadmill of a stair'; and it was Marduk who made the log-book of the sun's journey, and of the stars, when in the fifth tablet of *The Babylonian Creation* 'he projected positions for the Great Gods conspicuous in the sky, he gave them a starry aspect as constellations . . .'

One historian of religions has remarked that for the Chaldeans 'contemplation of the stars had become communion'; and Babylon in its later days was also the city of astrologers seeing archetypes in the constellations.

Nimbly, lightly, Babylon has passed from language to language, civilization to civilization, from Akkadian to Hebrew, Aramaic, Old Persian, Greek, Latin, Arabic, English, to all of them.

Nebuchadnezzar's prayer, 'May I attain eternal age', has been granted, after a fashion. In spite of his comparatively humane treatment of the Israelites he is remembered as the grand tyrant; because he desecrated the temple in Jerusalem he suffers the tauntings and blastings of the prophets. But while Nebuchadnezzar lives on his 'eternal age', Marduk is unknown; yet during the century of Babylon's great renaissance, from around 626 B.C. (and indeed from considerably earlier), Marduk was the source and symbol of the power and greatness of King and State. Whenever Babylon was defeated, whether by Sennacherib the Assyrian, or another of its enemies, the consummation of catastrophe was the carrying into exile of the statue of the god.

'Bel boweth down, Nebo stoopeth, their idols were upon the beasts and the cattle. ... They stoop, they bow down together, they could not deliver the burden but themselves are gone into captivity.' This probably refers to Sennacherib's conquest in 689 B.C., but it had happened many times before. The exile of the gods was a time of weakness and confusion. Marduk, or Bēl, 'the Lord', was necessary to Babylon, and the king was necessary to the god, for when the king was not present in Babylon at the New Year festival 'Marduk went not forth . . .' and the ceremonies were incomplete, even though *The Babylonian Creation* may have been chanted; so history and the poem are linked together.

What sort of writing is it then, this so-called 'Epic of Creation'?

It is not in the first place an epic at all, though often so called. It certainly does not conform, as the Gilgamesh poem does, to the definition of epic as 'narrative poetry that celebrates the achievements of some heroic personage of history or tradition'. It is nearer a 'mystery' in the sense of 'religious ordinance or rite'. It formed part of a liturgy and belonged to a particular occasion, the New Year festival at Babylon, and a particular place, the inner room or holy of holies of the god Marduk, where his statue lived throughout the year.

The text we have today is taken from tablets and fragments of tablets found at different times and places. The fullest, as with the Gilgamesh text, is late Assyrian and was found in the seventh-century library of Ashurbanipal at Nineveh. But other texts come from Ashur, an earlier Assyrian capital, and date from around 1000 B.C.; there are fragments from Kish and Uruk that are sixth-century, but all are copies of older originals. Though nothing has survived that is earlier than 1000 B.C., the real date of composition has in the past been thought to be 'Old Babylonian', that is early second millennium; but it is more likely to be principally a composition of the twelfth century.

The almost complete text is set out on seven tablets with an average of rather over 150 lines on each tablet, and with, at the beginning and end of each, a colophon copied from lost earlier versions. The first publication in 1876 was George Smith's *The Chaldean Account of Genesis*, and the latest and most complete is that of W. G. Lambert.[2]

Scholars have agreed that as 'literature' *The Babylonian Creation* is much inferior to *The Epic of Gilgamesh*, but this judgement may come partly from expecting something that was never intended. It plainly lacks the narrative excitement, the human situation and fairy-tale trappings; but these are no part of a great liturgical work, a mystery. The language has

2. 1967 (cuneiform only), and a forthcoming translation by the same.

been called archaic, full of obscure mythological allusions and Alexandrine elaboration; but this too may be unfair. It is impossible for us to feel the impact of such a text as it would have been experienced in sixth-century Babylon. What seem to us learned artificialities may have had a poetic resonance, and the persons may, like Keats's Titans, Malory's Arthur, Yeats's Deirdre and Cuchulain, have moved within a penumbra of religious and poetic allusion that is inaccessible to us. The style varies from that of cosmic beginnings, no more adorned than the 'book of the generations of Adam', through dialogue and description, which may be florid but is often powerful, to the punning and concision of the last hymn. Where so much is unknown an act of faith may be required to descry a poetic intention, 'a half-making out of the presence of poetry of an unexpected or unfamiliar kind . . .'[3]

The Babylonian Creation then is cast in the high style of the hymns. Like Hebrew poetry it has no rhyme nor alliteration, but the repetition of vowels within the line has sometimes an hypnotic insistence. The lines form couplets and quatrains, or longer 'stanzas'; each line is divided by a caesura and the half-lines have usually each a single accent, the final accent usually falling on the penultimate syllable:

enūma | élish || lā nabū | shamāmu

The single line may be a complete sentence of between four and seven words. As in Hebrew poetry the second half of a couplet or quatrain may echo the first in slightly different and heightened language giving a kind of rhythmic balance. In the fifth tablet, lines 133 to 136, we have for instance:

> Over these things that your hands have formed,
> who will administer law?
> Over all this earth that you have made,
> who is to sit in judgement?

3. Peter Levi, S. J., in *Agenda* (1968).

This suits sung or chanted poetry better than a 'literary' work. We know in fact, from a rubric to the liturgy, that *The Babylonian Creation* was recited aloud; though whether it was ever accompanied, or broken up into chorus and antiphon, as was sometimes done with other poems, we do not know. The early second-millennium poem called *The Exaltation of Inanna* has choruses, probably to be sung antiphonally; a Canaanite poem lays down that a passage shall be recited, or chanted, to the lute seven times, and the priests shall reply with the refrain.

We can make a guess as to how such chanting sounded for a traditional music was preserved by the Jewish communities in South Arabia and in Persia which is very ancient and has been claimed as 'almost as old as in the Babylonian community'.[4] Words are sung, not spoken, following Jewish law, several of the chants being exact counterparts of the Gregorian, which is again the 'supernatural' mode that Clement of Alexandria recommended to Christian singers in the second century. Such persistence of a technique is not intrinsically improbable for, as Imogen Holst points out in her study of *Tune*:

> Gregorian reciting-tones were made for use, not for ornament. As with street cries, their memorable patterns have grown from the practical need for making the human voice audible at a distance ... the laziest way of transforming speech into song is to chant each word on the same note ... [but this] is far more exhausting in the end, for it lacks the give-and-take of a two-note chant where the relaxation at the cadence stores up new energy for continuing.

4. A. Z. Idelsohn, 'Jewish Music', quoted by Imogen Holst, *Tune*, 196, p2. 43.

II

The Translation

The difficulty of choosing a suitable form for an English version of *The Babylonian Creation* is dismaying. Plain prose may do for narrative like *The Epic of Gilgamesh*, but hardly meets the needs of a liturgical poem with its formal structure dependent to some extent on ritual and didactic requirements, rather than the telling of a story. It should perhaps be in verse throughout – a sort of verse that could be chanted in the manner described; but this proved too difficult. The opening cosmogony has some of the magical properties of an incantation and *must* be in verse; also the final 'Hymn of the Fifty Names of Marduk'. The Hymn breaks naturally into short stanzas, name by name; although oddly these are not always the same as the breaks in the original text. Each name has a meaning: Lugal-Dimmer-Ankia is Lord-of-the-Gods-of-Heaven-and-Earth, like Cœur-de-Lion or Praise-God Barebones and Sorry-for-Sin. Some names are archaic and some are Joycean puns: Marukka, the second name or title, plays on both *mar*, to create, and *marru*, axe or hammer; so 'hammering out the whole creation' combines both ideas. Some of the names cannot be translated, and sometimes even when the parts that make up a name are known we are no nearer its real meaning. What, for instance, would a stranger to Western civilization with a basic knowledge of English make of the sentence: 'The chairman went into the boardroom'? Might he not see a carpenter going into a log-cabin?

For most of *The Babylonian Creation* I have rejected any standard verse form in favour of a sort of prose that is broken into short paragraphs, which sometimes, but not always, correspond to the verse divisions of the original (for these often cut across speech and sense, so that I have been ruled by the latter rather than an exact reproduction of the divisions in the text). There are some other points at which verse is required. The creation of man is one of these, for this again is magic, a form of incantation. Occasionally the order of lines has been inverted, all the repetitions are retained, and in the opening cosmogony, where the names would have been understood by all who heard them as meaning 'sky' or 'silt', I have worked the meaning into the text.

SUMMARY TABLE

Tablet	Events of Creation	New Year Festival
I	Prelude: Cosmogony	Evening of the fourth day
	Birth of Marduk	The Babylonian Creation chanted
	Creation of Tiamat's horde	
II	First failure against Tiamat	
	Marduk is summoned and bargains with Anshar	
III	First assembly of the gods	Ceremonial of the eighth of Nisan in Ubshukinna [?]
	Marduk is given his destiny	
IV	First enthronement of Marduk	Procession to the Festival House on the tenth day [?]
	First banquet of the gods	
	The arming of Marduk (gods disperse [?])	
	Marduk's battle with Tiamat and victory	
V	Marduk organizes the universe	Celebration in the Festival House [?]
	The gods bring presents	
	Assembly of the gods	
	Marduk's second enthronement	
	Marduk announces his plan for the building of Babylon	

Tablet	Events of Creation	New Year Festival
VI	Creation of Man	Return from the Festival
	Organization of the divine Hierarchy by Marduk	House on the eleventh day and second great
	The Anunnaki gods set to work for a year to build Babylon and Marduk's temple	assembly in Ubshukinna
	(Gods disperse [?])	
	Second great banquet and exaltation of the victorious weapons	
	Marduk's destiny ratified	
	Short hymn of praise, and beginning of the Hymn of the Fifty Names of Marduk	
VII	Hymn of the Fifty Names of Marduk continued	
	Epilogue	

III

Nabū-bēlshu, the son of Naʾid-Marduk, the son of a smith, wrote it for the life of his soul, and the life of his house and deposited it in the temple Ezida

Colophon to Tablet IV of Enuma elish

In this section of the Introduction I shall give a brief synopsis of *The Babylonian Creation*, and follow it with an investigation into some of the conceptions underlying it, which may turn out to be rather less alien and peculiar than appears at first sight; for that some *are* alien and even repellent cannot be denied.

This poem, this liturgy, begins in chaos and ends in an orderly universe governed by a hierarchy of powers; it is therefore a creation, of a sort, although not at all as in the biblical Genesis. In the account of beginnings the first gods come into existence within a watery chaos, which is itself a god, and the names they bear explain the growth of the universe. In fact there are two uncreated primeval beings, Ti'āmat and Apsū, that represent water and inertia in different aspects; and there is a third beside these called Mummu. From, or within, these three there appear a pair of gods, male and female, Lahmu and Lahāmu; the names mean silt. After them come Anshar and Kishar, meaning the two horizons of sky and earth; and they are separated by the birth of Anu, the heavens, and of his son Ea-Nudimmud, god of earth and its waters and of wisdom. This prelude is followed by conflict; there is war in heaven, and a gradual victory of law and order over anarchy and the uncontrolled wasting of energy. Ea, representing the younger gods, defeats Apsu and Mummu, through intellectual power and his peculiar 'wisdom'. After Apsu her husband is defeated, Tiamat is roused by her angry children. She takes a new husband, Kingu, whom she sets at their head, and she creates a horde of monsters to fight beside them.

Before this happens the grand theme of the poem has been introduced with the birth of Marduk, the son of Ea, the marvellous child endowed with supreme beauty, strength and wisdom. When Ea and Anshar fail against Tiamat, Marduk is called to be the champion of the gods. He summons their full assembly, but first he drives a hard bargain. If he is to take on Tiamat and her horde he must be king and absolute ruler of all the other gods, which means ruler of 'heaven and earth', the universe, for all eternity.

Marduk defeats Tiamat, not because he is stronger, but because he is better armed. He immediately sets about the exercise of his new powers. From the body of Tiamat he constructs the earth and the waters: rivers, springs and wells; he sets up laws governing the operations of the sun, moon and stars, and puts the rebel gods to labour in the service of the victors. The great assembly is summoned a second time, and the whole scene contracts suddenly from the unlocalized regions of the cosmic 'beginning' to a point on earth, Babylon, this city, this exact spot where the poem is chanted, at this one particular moment in time. Here, at the centre of the earth, the gods agree to build a temple and tower for Marduk, as an image of heaven and a place for them to meet together at the New Year, as they were to do during all the years of Babylon's greatness. The statues of the gods came each spring from other Babylonian cities, rowed through the canals and down the rivers, to meet in Marduk's temple, where destinies were settled, and the world set on its way for another twelvemonth.

In the poem, when this has been done, almost as an afterthought man is created; and he is created a slave in the service of the gods. These are the two great interlocking themes of our poem: the story and triumph of Marduk and the 'Settling of Destinies', first by all the gods when they appoint Marduk their king, and secondly by Marduk himself in exercise of his unique prerogative. The poem ends with a long hymn to Marduk of some 180 lines, which may not have been part of the original poem. At this point Marduk has engrossed the powers and virtue of all the other gods. A gesture towards monotheism that progressed no farther.

The Babylonian Creation, with its repetitions and disjointed action, seems at first sight to have little form, but this is not really so. There is an alternation of active and static parts. After the prelude there are two conflicts followed by two assemblies and a final confirmation of 'destinies', and then the long paean of praise. The table on p. 20 shows the organization of the poem, its disposition on the seven tablets, and its connection with the eleven-day programme of the New Year festival (see also below p. 44). This form is less literary than symphonic. The repetitions of the set speeches and descriptions belong to music; accordingly the cosmogony acts as a short prelude; both the main themes are repeated and developed, and the 'Hymn of the Fifty Names' is a long coda. The impression all through is of some sort of performance.

The cosmogony at the beginning is an imaginary model or metaphor, like explanations of the beginning of the universe in popular physics and astronomy. Without such a model the human mind cannot even *begin* to think about the universe; but behind this particular model there lie not only an elaborate temple ritual, but many hundreds of years of religious thinking.

There were other cosmogonies, some already known to the Sumerian inhabitants of Mesopotamia two thousand years before Nebuchadnezzar II. They all form a background to our text. Many of the names of the gods and the epithets are direct translations from the Sumerian language. It was always good to begin a religious text with a cosmogony; it fixed the ceremony or spell or healing, or whatever the occasion was, into the order of eternal things. It tapped the spiritual power stored and latent in the surrounding world and gave extra potency to whatever followed. A charm for curing a toothache was introduced by one well-known cosmogony, and the whole of the *Adapa* myth was preserved into the seventh century as an incantation against disease. The *Atra-hasīs Epic*, which describes a conflict of gods, creation of man, and the sending of the flood, appears to have been designed specially for the use of midwives; it therefore gives a very different account of man from that of *Enuma elish*. The Sumerians also had a very ancient creation myth that began in a garden and used a primitive sort of biological language. Since the avowed purpose of *The Babylonian Creation* was to establish an absolute monarchy and to re-establish a world order that would endure for the next year, it is naturally far more concerned with matters of government and hierarchies; and since Babylon was 'an image of the moving heavens' much of it lays down laws for sun, moon, stars and seasons. This advanced and sophisticated apparatus goes side by side with the old Sumerian topography, the landscape of long ago.

The inhabitants of Lower Mesopotamia in the fourth and

third millennia, when these ideas were probably becoming articulate, lived in a flat world of marsh and lagoon reaching to the horizon, and only broken by the darker horizontal lines of the alluvial mud-banks and the forest of reeds. It was a landscape which wind and storm could suddenly blot out, and on to which the sun blazed without shade or shelter through the long months of summer. There was a tempestuous north wind and a scorching south wind that was feared; there was no divine mountain, no Olympos of the gods; heaven was the tall sky above the most towering clouds. In fact another sort of landscape must have been remembered, since the Sumerian word *kur*, meaning 'earth' or 'world', was the same as the word for 'mountain' and later for 'foreign land'; but mountains, rocks and valleys have little place in *The Babylonian Creation* except as a heavy weight to keep down the waters under the earth.

In physical terms then the first state of the universe at the beginning of this poem is that misty watery chaos from which the land of Lower Mesopotamia was never far removed, and which it was felt might return at any time. Into this wet world silt was deposited like the sand-banks deposited by the great rivers, and these it was that defined the two unbroken circles, the horizons of the sky and of earth. None of this is very far from that view of earth as the 'watery planet' which our astronauts, looking back from the moon, have seen as a blue and white bubble swirling with clouds and water. Moreover it is geologically sound since three quarters of the earth's surface *is* water, and nine tenths of the water is in the deep ocean which geographers call 'the Abyss', and which drops to depths of over 36,000 feet.

Tiamat is a proper name, which can occasionally mean any stretch of water, sea or lake. Apsu is the semitic form of Sumerian Abzu, both meaning the ocean, the abyss and also the uttermost limit. The Greeks expressed the bottomless and unfathomable as ἄβυσσος, from βυσσός or βυθός, the deep of the sea. The same thought was expressed mythologically as Tartaros, Erebos. Any similarity between Greek ἄβυσσος, from which we have 'abyss', and 'Abzu' or 'Apsu' is pure coincidence, but 'abyss' will do very well as a translation. The Oxford Dictionary describes it as: 'the great deep, the primal chaos; the bowels of the earth; the infernal pit . . .'; also 'a bottomless gulf; any unfathomable cavity or void space . . .' and, at last, Herschel's 'awful abyss which separates us from the stars'. This covers all the senses in which the Babylonians understood Apsu and Tiamat, except the anthropomorphic ones, in which they speak and act at the beginning of *The Babylonian Creation*.

It is this last sense which makes them so difficult to visualize. But it is this trying to visualize concretely, and describe, that probably creates the difficulty when we face these vast ambiguous figures of the early world. On one plane Tiamat is a female creature with eyes, nostrils and entrails; a mother with paps and sex, all apparently in the human mould. But she is also a moist monster, a vast mollusc that separates like a clam to form the arc of heaven and the ring of earth. Identification of Tiamat with the dragon is mistaken. She is the bitter water of ocean and she is also in some way the sweet waters under the earth which well up as springs and rivers to reach the fields and villages of men. In this latter form she can still become a menacing force: the flood from the north when the Tigris and Euphrates, full of melting snow, sweep down to inundate the flat plains of Mesopotamia. But she is something more than this: she is inertia, mere formlessness, the ground of the universe.

Apsu, the husband of Tiamat, seems to be a more creative power, but creation is flawed by discord; the mingling of the waters, the sweet and the bitter, did not lead to fusion but to fission. In his anthropomorphic *persona* Apsu is unattractive.

He desires to lie quiet and do nothing; but when sleep is made impossible by the overflow of undirected energy among gods by himself created, he is ready to kill them all. Tiamat, on the other hand, is the lazy and indulgent mother, ready to ignore her troublesome brood. Apsu seeks sleep, Tiamat the stupor of inertia. When the conflict of the gods leads to the death of Apsu, Tiamat is startled into creativity; but left to herself she can only make monsters, the proper progeny of chaos.

The third person of this primordial trinity is Mummu. The exact meaning of the name is unknown but it has been interpreted physically as mist or cloud, while the late Neo-Platonic philosopher Damascius knew of a Moymis or Mumis the 'only begotten son' of Apsu and Tiamat, whom he took to be 'the mental world' νοητὸς κόσμος, or *logos*.

In the early second-millennium *Myth of Zū* there is a hint of another meaning. Zu was the semitic name for the Sumerian *Imdugud*, which means something like 'flashing wind'; this was the great storm-wind which was represented as an eagle with a lion's head. Like Kingu in our poem he stole the 'Tablets of Fate', but was defeated by Ningirsu, originally a much greater god than Marduk. In the battle between them an arrow speeding from the bow is ordered to return to its *mummu*, which means that the shaft becomes again part of the living cane from which it was cut, the gut returns to the animal's rump and the feathers to the bird's wings. In cosmic terms this is a return to the womb of chaos, and in twentieth-century language it could stand for the second law of thermodynamics, matter degenerating through loss of energy to its simplest common denominator, so leading in the end to 'a run-down universe'; we could therefore understand *mummu* as 'entropy'. The early Greek philosophers are said by Aristotle to have conceived of a universal first principle, 'that from which a thing first comes-into-being and into which it is finally destroyed', and this is

27

not far removed from the last meaning of *mummu*.[5] This makes Mummu a very difficult name to express in English, but I have tried to imply his various aspects.

If we pursue Mummu a little further through the action of the poem we find him overpowered by Ea, confined and locked away. Ea, in his creative capacity, checks entropy, and when he binds Apsu and Mummu, he reverses the whole process of degeneration.

At the end of the poem all three primordial existences, Tiamat–Apsu–Mummu, have been defeated; they are 'dead' or, like Mummu, locked away. But for the Babylonians the material world was eternal; nothing is ever wasted in this thrifty universe, not even death. We know this also from Diodorus Siculus, the Greek geographer who was born in the first century B.C. 'The Chaldeans say that the substance of the world is eternal, and that it neither has a first beginning nor . . . will at a later time suffer destruction.' At the end of *The Babylonian Creation* the 'dead' existences still exist, but now they are part of a coherent cosmos.

Throughout this prelude the language reflects the watery tempestuous nature of the beings it describes, as it does again whenever Tiamat is called up. If this is what the ancient Babylonians imagined cosmic beginning to have been like, in the language of myth, the scale and scope of the thing imagined is not so far from what we know in the language of fact, of the early history of the earth; that time when the gases of the atmosphere and the waters of the ocean were still locked up, to be released during millions of years of earthquake and

5. G. Kirk and J. Raven, *The Presocratic Philosophers*, 1966, p. 87; for the *Myth of Zu*, with new texts, see *Ancient Near Eastern Texts Relating to the Old Testament*, 1955, p. 515, and Thorkild Jacobsen in *Religions in Antiquity*, seminar edited by J. Neusner, Comparative Studies Center, Dartmouth College, New Hampshire, 1966, where he interprets *mummu* as 'original form'.

eruption, flinging clouds of carbon dioxide, nitrogen and vapour out from the boiling surface. From these vapours eventually there was formed an impenetrable dark atmosphere that surrounded the earth in obscurity darker than the darkest days we know. This state apparently lasted until the earth was cool enough for the vapour to condense, and for rain to fall. At first the surface was too hot and the water was turned back into gas; but when the earth had cooled then the great rains began, and went on for hundreds of years out of a pitch black atmosphere. The water lay in hollows and depressions of the earth's surface till gradually the oceans were formed, and at last the clouds thinned, and for the first time the sun shone on a blue sea that already covered the greater part of the earth. That is a geologist's model of the early earth, based on the known behaviour of gases and liquids, beside which we set the poetic model based on what the Babylonians knew of wind and weather and the natural world; the world of Apsu and Tiamat, gaseous, watery, indistinct; of the loosing of immense stores of inchoate energy in the first conflict, the separation of upper and nether waters, the pervading darkness, and the ultimate triumph of the sun-god shining down on an earth where land and ocean are already divided and the stars are visible at night keeping their courses, the guarantors of universal order.

The Babylonian cosmogony is oddly lopsided. After the creation of Anu, the heavens, we would expect to hear of earth, its features and creatures; but the wife of Anu is never named, and Ea, his only son, is another watery god. Earth does not appear until after the death of Tiamat four tablets later. The intervening material has been taken up with the birth of Marduk and his story. This asymmetry is probably due to the liturgical occasion of the performance within the programme of the New Year festival at Babylon. This was above all a time of cosmic renewal when the whole natural and divine order – sun, moon, stars and all their gods – were confirmed in their natures and functions; the moment, both in time and out of time, when the cosmic order was secured with the participation of king, priests and, in a lesser degree, people. So, even though gods have consorts in *The Babylonian Creation*, the latter play an entirely minor role, and this too is no doubt because of the masculine, cosmic, political nature of the occasion.

Anu is the ordinary name for the sky: he is the heavens, the zenith, the heir and supplanter of his father Anshar; but, until the apotheosis of Marduk, Anshar retains the greater authority. It is Anshar who sends out first Ea, then Anu, to encounter Tiamat; but, from the advice that Ea gives his son Marduk when he is summoned by Anshar, we guess that there is still something dangerous, primeval and unpredictable about Anshar. He flies into rages; his own children approach him with circumspection. Though it is never explicitly said, he must have fathered the contumacious rebellious gods, as well as the 'establishment' gods. Perhaps he gets his character from the fact that it is from the horizon that storms and thunder, darkness and gales approach, not out of the height of heaven. Anu represents authority. It was his authority that was usurped by Kingu, and he was the original owner of the Tables of Destiny, the outward visible sign of universal order and government; but Marduk was the great god of Babylon and the hero of the poem and there was no room left for Anu within its framework except as his 'father', that is forefather. Nevertheless when Marduk leaves to meet Tiamat the authority with which he is armed by the assembled gods is 'the will of Anu', 'the word of command, the word from heaven [Anu]'. It was Anu who gave him the net in which he held Tiamat, and it was Anu who set him on the throne and who presided over his apotheosis.

The Babylonian Creation does not tell us when or how the rebellious gods were created, only that 'discord broke out among the gods although they were brothers'. Sometimes they are called Anunnaki, though not apparently when in flagrant revolt: then they are the 'fallen' or 'rebel' gods, the adversary. As such they are contrasted with 'the gods his fathers', referring to Marduk and his close kindred. Sometimes too they are contrasted with the Igigi, who are especially gods of heaven; the Anunnaki usually lived in the underworld. The dichotomy is not invariable and in some early texts Annunaki and Igigi are synonymous. In the poem of *Inanna's Journey to Hell* the seven Anunnaki inhabit hell and pronounce judgement on the doomed (see p. 122).

The monsters created by Tiamat have names well known in Mesopotamian religion: like the man-scorpion, and the *bashmu* (Sumerian *ushum-gal*), sometimes translated as hydra and represented as a many-headed serpent. After the defeat of Tiamat, as part of the organization of the universe, Marduk allots a place for the eleven monsters 'with the weapons of war broken he bound to his foot the eleven. . . . He made likenesses of them, and now they stand at the gate of the abyss, at the Apsu Gate.'

This may mean that they were represented in relief at the entrance to the Apsu temple in Eridu (the ancient Sumerian city on the edge of a great tidal lake), which was on another level the entrance to the pit. That this was actually so cannot be proved, but an analogy is the famous Dragon of Babylon, the *sirrush*, that could be seen any day in turquoise-coloured tiles striding over the Ishtar Gate at the north end of the processional way in Babylon itself, and can, for that matter, still be seen in Berlin, where the whole gate was rebuilt by Koldewey.

Ea has taken the place of the Sumerian god Enki, Lord Earth, originally the god of the whole earth. Sometimes he lived at the bottom of the sea, and it was his temple in Eridu that was called the Abzu, the abyss. In *The Babylonian Creation* we realize how the dizzying distances of Abzu or Apsu can be identical with an ordinary brick temple, for the temple is the mundane counterpart of the palace that Ea built in heaven in the first tablet of *The Babylonian Creation*. The worship of Enki in Eridu is far older than anything in the Babylonian poem. He is water, especially in its relationship to man, and in its beneficent aspect: the springs, rivers, lakes and the sea full of fish for fishermen. A god of wisdom, he is also the great magician, source of creativeness and of many inventions. The *usrat* created by Ea to overcome Apsu is both a powerful spell and an intellectual design; it is an adumbration of the form of the universe which does not yet exist but which may exist – a first germ of the great plan of an ordered cosmos to be consummated by Marduk, the son whom Ea will beget. It is a difficult word to translate, but 'artifice' may suggest the fragility of something that still belongs to the world of thought.

At two points the language of this poem betrays the fact that Ea himself was originally the creator of mankind, as he is in the *Atrahasis Epic*. Near the beginning of the sixth tablet we have, 'When it was done, when Ea in his wisdom had created man . . .', and at the end of the Hymn of Praise of the seventh tablet we see again clearly, behind the young hero, the older god. Ea says, 'The Great Gods have glorified my son, he is Ea, named by name, he will execute my will and direct my rites.' Ea has a wife, Damkina, and their son is born into a simple family, though perhaps an idealized one.

With the birth of Marduk we enter on the central theme of the poem; we also add a political dimension to the cosmic one. The name 'marduk' means sun-child, or son-of-the-sun, and carries with it more of the glory of light than the brightness that is simply an attribute of divinity itself. He has some of the character both of sun and storm, and in the final Hymn of Praise he is given, or lent, the name and character of almost all the other gods. For the purposes of that hymn and that occasion, he represents in himself the entire pantheon. His rôle in *The*

Babylonian Creation is the familiar one of the young god who surpasses and supplants his elders. Historically he wears other gods' shoes. In the eternal battle between cosmos and chaos other and greater heroes had killed monsters, when Babylon and its god were still of no account in the world.

Enlil, who was air and storm and active power, and who usually stood second after Anu in authority among the gods, plays very little part in *The Babylonian Creation*, and this is because he was himself the hero of just such another contest. At the end of the 'Hymn of the Fifty Names' in a voluntary act of abdication he bestows on Marduk the last title of the fifty: *Bēl Mātāti*, Lord of the Land, or Lord of This World, his own name.

There is a Sumerian poem in which Enki or Ea fought against the nether waters. It comes in a cosmogonic incantation or charm introducing a longer poem, like the cosmogony at the beginning of *The Babylonian Creation*:

When the world was filled with the waters of chaos,
When the firmament was parted from the earth,
When earth was parted from the firmament,
When the name of mankind was established,
When Anu took for himself the heavens,
When Enlil took for himself the earth,
When Ereshkigal had taken the Underworld for her portion
   (*or* had been carried off by the Underworld [*kur*])
When Enki set sail for the Underworld
Against the king the small ones stormed,
Against Enki the great ones were hurled,
Like stones, the small and great ones hurled,
At the boat's keel, the boat of Enki,
A raging tempest, attacking,
At the bows like a jackal the water devours,
Against Enki like a lion it rends the stern.

(trans. Kramer, Jacobsen, etc.)

In another Sumerian liturgy it is Ninurta, sometimes the south wind and the son of Enlil, who battles with the primeval underground flood. Like Marduk he is armed with a net and with the whirlwind or tornado, and like Marduk he piles rocks over the defeated waters and a mountain to hold them back. He too irrigates the land, leading the rivers into the safe channel of the Tigris. The result of these victories is always the blessing of fertility: herbs, wine, honey, trees, cattle, gold and silver.

Until early in the second millennium Marduk was the patron and local god of an unimportant town on the Euphrates. But when little Babylon became Babylon the Great, with the rise of the first Amorite (semitic) dynasty, the dynasty of which Hammurabi the law-giver was the third king, then all this was changed. The claims and stature of the city god grew blow by blow, with those of the city, for the politics of heaven and the society of the gods reflect society and politics on earth. The second millennium was a restless period of war between states and of barbarian invasions. The first dynasty of Babylon survived for a little more than two hundred years; and though Marduk was very great in the eyes of the Babylonians they did not yet claim for him authority over the great gods of the old Sumerian cities: Nippur, Eridu and Uruk. Professor Lambert, writing of the rise of Marduk, sees it as a slow progress, with his universal supremacy delayed until the twelfth century B.C., during what is called the Middle Babylonian period. After this time names compounded with 'Marduk' become usual for kings of Babylon. The immediate cause of the apotheosis of Marduk may have been, according to Lambert, the triumphant return of the god's statue from captivity in Elam, after the defeat of this powerful eastern neighbour and traditional enemy of Babylon by Nebuchadnezzar I. This would also have been a likely time for the composition of the poem of *The Babylonian Creation* in its present form as a great

Hymn of Praise to a triumphant Marduk.[6] In time Marduk himself was challenged by even younger heroes. When Assyria became a great power threatening Babylonia, the city god of Ashur supplanted Marduk in the northern capital, and his name appears in place of Marduk's in the Assyrian text of *The Babylonian Creation*. At Ashur the king of Assyria was portrayed on the bronze doors of a temple in the rôle of Tiamat's conqueror; so close was the interdependence of state religion and of politics.

In *The Babylonian Creation* Marduk is the model ruler. He is beautiful, strong, brave, wise and not without subtlety as a politician. His handling of the assembly of gods is positively machiavellian. In early Mesopotamia the city-states were ruled by councils or assemblies, but in times of emergency the assembly would nominate one leading citizen to act for them as king, and as general to lead the army; then as soon as the danger was over the council reassumed authority. When Marduk stipulates that he shall be elected king *for ever*, and have authority over the whole universe, this is something quite different. When the gods agree in the assembly they draw up the blueprint for an absolute monarchy. The business of the mortal king is the defence of his realm, the support of law and order and the provision of everything needed by the people and the gods. So Marduk, as the divine prototype, as soon as the danger is over, sets about organizing the universe for the greater comfort of himself and the other gods. Finally through his identification with Ea or Enki he becomes the creator of man.

In Genesis man is the crown of creation. Here on the other

6. W. G. Lambert in *The Seed of Wisdom*, ed. W. S. McCulloch, 1964, p. 3. The idea of a west-semitic Syro-Palestinian Marduk, based on his characteristics as a storm-god rather than a god of sun and light, has been revived recently by T. Jacobsen, but would need more powerful argument to support it.

hand he is an afterthought; substitute labour for the rebel gods. He is formed from the arterial blood of the arch-criminal and leader of the rebellion, Kingu. This name seems to stand, in Sumerian, for some sort of unskilled labourer. Compared with the other gods he is only fit to serve. Though Tiamat chose him out from among the first generation of her children to be her second consort, he was a failure as a leader of revolt; and even the Tables of Destiny which she bound on to his breast did him no good. Unqualified, and a usurper, he could not profit from his high position. There is black humour in making this creature the source of the best part in man. 'Blood to blood' and 'blood to bone' man is made up from the dead Kingu. I suspect a deliberate lopsidedness here, just as there is in the story of cosmic beginnings, and for the same reason. Only those matters have been chosen that are relevant to the observance of the New Year festival. In the early second-millennium *Atrahasis Epic* man is created from a dead god, and the god's name is Wē-ila, or Hasisu, which has some connection with 'wisdom' or 'reason'. Enki is the creator, with the help of the Great Mother who mixes the clay with the blood and flesh, 'so that god and man shall be mingled'. Clay represents the wholly material part, while blood is the source of animal life, and the god's *flesh* is the mortal spirit and reason of a man, his life till death. But the god's *spirit* escapes, for if man possessed that he would himself be god. A crucial line seems to say: 'A soul shall inhabit the flesh, and she [the goddess] shall cause him to live and life shall be his nature.'[7]

The creation of a prototype man, with his higher nature and potential, is followed by a sort of mass production of men and women in clay moulds. The reason for their creation is the same as in our poem – that man should labour instead of

7. W. G. Lambert and A. R. Millard, *Atra-hasis, The Babylonian Story of the Flood*, 1969; and J. Finkelstein in *Religions in Antiquity*, ed. J. Neusner, Dartmouth College, 1966, pp. 92 f.

the gods: 'I have made him a coolie carrying baskets of earth.'
These differing accounts do not necessarily cancel each other
out. The Atrahasis creation was part of a ritual for midwives;
it preserves the midwife's lore, and has none of the cosmic
purpose of *The Babylonian Creation* in which man, as man, is
quite unimportant. It belongs to a different set of needs and
circumstances. The things omitted do not imply that in
Babylon man was thought of as any less subtle an individual.

The second major theme of *The Babylonian Creation*, after
that of glorifying Marduk, is the ritual known as 'Fixing the
Destinies'. Three times in the course of the poem the gods
come together in full assembly (or if they were present at the
creation of man it would be four times), and this summoning
of gods into solemn synod was enacted at least twice during the
New Year festival in Babylon on the eighth and eleventh days
(see the Table on p. 20, and p. 44). They met in a particular
room, in the temple, named the *Ubshukinna*, after the 'Room
of Destiny' at Nippur, the ancient religious centre of Sumeria,
which was itself an earthly counterpart of the meeting-place
in heaven where heavenly destinies were fixed.

The Akkadian word *shimtu* means rather more than we
mean by destiny, lot or fate; nor is it 'providence'. It includes
the physical appearance, attributes and influence – the whole
nature – of a person or a thing (for objects like precious stones
have their *shimtu*); and it includes their place in the great design
of the universe. To 'fix destinies' is to have power, not only
over events, but over the physical nature of the world. This
power was thought to reside in the Tables or Tablets of
Destiny, and when these fell into wrong hands the effect was
total catastrophe and a reversal of the natural order: the world
was stood upon its head. At the beginning of the cosmogony
the state of indeterminacy and chaos or inertia is expressed as
a time before the gods had been given names, and before their
respective *shimata* had been established. Meaning so many

things, it is another almost impossible word to translate. By saying 'the gods were nameless, natureless, futureless' I do not think I have got nearer than an approximation.

In the course of the poem the power of destiny is transferred from the assembly to one person, Marduk. On the earthly plane that part of the New Year ceremonial which is concerned with Fixing the Destinies is supremely important to man. It is a ratification and prolongation of the *status quo* which assures mankind that the dangerous powers that lie in fire and heat shall not get out of hand; limits are imposed on the sun so that it shall not shine too long or, dropping too low, shall not destroy the earth. Mountains are piled on Tiamat so that the underground waters shall rise gently as springs and wells. Even so the danger is not removed once and for ever. Floods can still come raging down from the north, to blot out villages and cities; or the sea may brim over the sand-banks of the south and flood the maritime plain, 'the deserts of the sea' as the Authorized Version names them. These are the powers represented by Tiamat and the monsters of her creation. Continual mental and ritual activity were needed simply to hold the world in equilibrium. Marduk's battle must be fought year after year. Tiamat is never entirely conquered. Almost the last verses of the Hymn of Praise exhort – they do not command – Tiamat to

> recede into the future
> far off from mankind,
> till time is old . . .

After our fashion we know the same fears, with our ambivalent relationship to nuclear power, to chemical poison and biological weapons and all the potentials of science and technology for good and bad; these are never mastered by us, nor is our environment any more neutral than that of the ancient inhabitants of Mesopotamia, even though unlike them we suppose ourselves to be the authors of our own dreadful powers.

IV

O Bel, your dwelling is the city of Babylon.

Such is the shape of the great Babylonish poem. The mundane scene of its enactment is identical with the divine scene of action. Earth mirrors heaven, and the earthly liturgy echoes the heavenly. *Ubshukinna,* the Chamber of Destiny, timeless, divine, is also a room of Marduk's brick palace beside the Euphrates; a mound of earth in which you can dirty your shoes today. The great *ziggurat* of Babylon was called the *Etemenanki,* the 'House of the Foundation of Heaven and Earth', the common term for the whole universe, which indeed it was; just as the parts of Solomon's temple on the rock of Jerusalem *were* the cosmos: water, earth and heaven.

So much is known about the New Year spring festival at Babylon that we can go a long way towards reconstructing the actual scene when, on the evening of the fourth day of the month Nisan (April), the priest of Marduk stood in an inner room alone in front of the figure of the god, to chant the entire creation poem. This knowledge comes from the excavation of the buildings, from texts which describe the buildings, and from one most important text which, though incomplete, gives the rubric of the liturgy for the first five days of the festival, with many of the prayers and hymns.

Until the last year of the nineteenth century Babylon was a wilderness, a scatter of Arab huts among little hills, built from the bricks of the ancient city, which for centuries had served as a quarry for building materials. From time to time

it was visited by travellers, and some of the first cuneiform
writing to be seen in Europe was brought back from Babylon
by an Italian traveller early in the seventeenth century. In 1835
another traveller was writing to a friend: 'Babylon in all its
desolation is a sight not so awful as that of the human mind in
ruins.'

In 1899 serious excavation began under R. Koldewey, and
from then until the beginning of the First World War the
massive work went ahead uninterrupted. Not very much has
been found of the oldest city, but much has survived of the
great city of the Neo-Babylonian renaissance, from 626 to
539 B.C. The Euphrates then flowed further east than today,
and passed immediately under the walls of the large temple-
complex of Marduk, called the *Esagīla*. The plan on p. 10 will
clarify the description that follows. The river and its linked
system of canals was the great highway. It was by river and
canal that the statues of the gods came to Babylon on the fifth
day of the New Year festival, and the procession of the tenth
day was also partly by boat. The river divided the new town
on the west bank from the older and more sacred city on the
east. It was spanned by a many-arched bridge at a point
opposite Marduk's temple. This was separated from the court
of the stepped *ziggurat* by a line of buildings. The *ziggurat* was
seventy-five metres high with a triple stairway leading to a
small temple on top. Though it played no part in the New
Year festival (as far as that can be reconstructed), the *ziggurat*
must have dominated the whole city, visible from all its parts.

Herodotus saw and described it and Alexander was planning
to rebuild it when he died in 323 B.C. When the German
excavators started work it was a little hill, but since then it has
been quarried away for modern buildings, and today the tallest
and proudest monument of Babylon is a bank of mud in a
watery depression. It has returned to the water, silt and reeds
of the first lines of the Babylonian cosmogony.

Through the centre of the city ran the processional way, a straight line from the temple of Marduk north to the Ishtar Gate and beyond. This *via sacra* was a street of unparalleled magnificence, paved with red and white marble slabs brought from great distances. Its brick walls were faced with blue lapis lazuli glaze, the forerunner of all those blue mosques and palaces of western Asia; and there were friezes of bulls, lions and dragons in relief, coloured with red, white, yellow and lapis lazuli. At the towering Ishtar Gate there were nine rows of animals, yellow-gold bulls with blue manes and tufts, and green horns, and yellow lions flecked with white, all on a blue background. Nebuchadnezzar II boasted that he had made 'for the amazement of all people' the high-lying glistening road and the mighty superstructure.

Inside the Ishtar Gate, between the processional way and the river on the west, was the *Qasr*, the castle palace of Nebuchadnezzar, where the hanging gardens were. Beyond the gate the city stretched out towards the country with orchards and gardens, like all the cities of the Middle East; and somewhere out there among them, probably not very far away, was the *Bīt Akītu*, the Festival House, where an important part of the ritual took place. The corresponding *Bit Akitu* at the Assyrian capital of Ashur was 200 metres outside the gates, surrounded by beautiful watered gardens. It had a great court planted with trees and shrubs, and its bronze doors showed in relief the king setting out in his chariot to encounter Tiamat. It is fair to suppose that the original of this building, at Babylon, was not altogether unlike it.

The greater part of Marduk's temple, the *Esagila*, has been excavated and the empty dusty ruin (uncovered by the excavators) can be furnished out with descriptions preserved on contemporary tablets. An *esagila* is mentioned at the very end of the third millennium by Shulgi of Ur, and in the eighteenth century B.C. statues of Marduk and of Sarpanit, his consort, already existed at Babylon. Thereafter there were many burnings and lootings, and Marduk was carried away by enemies, and the temple lost its virtue. The last destruction was by Xerxes in 482 B.C., and the last mention of the *Esagila* is in 93 B.C. The plan of the temple is like many others in Mesopotamia; nothing could be less like a Greek temple or like the basilicas and cathedrals of Europe. There is a courtyard or courtyards surrounded by numbers of intercommunicating rooms of different sizes, but none very large, and with corridors and smaller courts. Such a plan explains those references in the poem to the chapels and chambers of the different gods: each had his own within the larger complex. Superficially, at least, the plan is closer to certain great Islamic buildings such as the Friday Mosque in Isphahan, or even like that of an Oxford college, with gods of lesser or greater importance in the place of fellows, a great hall for feasting and fixing fates, and a master's lodging of particular beauty and importance; in this case the chambers of the master of gods, Marduk.

Marduk's own suite was dramatically arranged. If you entered the temple complex by the great east door, the door used in the processions, this took you through a long chamber and out into the central court at a point where immediately facing you was the doorway into Marduk's chambers: first the *antecella*, then the *cella* with the niche for the god's statue. This was so placed in the middle of the long back wall that if all doors were open you could see straight through to it from the other side of the court; although little light would have penetrated so far, unless the hall was lit with torches. This hall was some 80 feet long by 25, and we know that once it glowed with alabaster and lapis lazuli that covered the lower parts of the walls, and that the ceiling glittered with plaques of gold and precious gems. Of the great treasure of the *Esagila* a few slips of lapis lazuli are all that have been found, though one, appropriately, shows Marduk standing on the waters, wearing a long tunic covered with hundreds of stars, and three great discs hanging from a chain round his neck. He is crowned with a tower-like tiara with plumes on top, he holds a ring, a sceptre and a sickle-shaped instrument, and at his feet crouches the dragon, the *sirrush*. It is a portrayal of the triumphant Marduk of the sixth tablet of creation. This dragon is a brisk, rather engaging creature with a serpent's head and scales, and a tail armed with the sting of a scorpion in the tip, a forked tongue, and the erect horns of the Arabian viper. The name means 'walking serpent' and the slim feline forelegs are more like a cheetah's than a lion's, while the hindlegs have an eagle's claws. It is Marduk's peculiar beast and, like Horace Walpole's earthquake, it is so gentle 'you could stroke it'. Close to Marduk's chambers were those of Sarpanit or Beltiya, his consort, and further off, grouped round the courtyard, those of Anu and Enlil and Ea. Because the last was identified later with Serapis, a healing god, it was probably here that Alexander's generals, Python and Seleukos, slept when they tried to learn by dreams, if they could, whether they should bring the dying emperor to the god for healing.

The Hall of Assembly, *Ubshukinna*, may have been in a part of the buildings that has never been fully excavated. One of the contemporary tablets describing the temple sets out a form of pilgrimage, which was to be followed from door to door and room to room. It started at the Door of the Flood, or Water Gate; from there the pilgrim walked round to the Door of the Guardian God, where he received a blessing, and passed on to the principal door, the Door of the Sunrise; from there through the Door of the Salutation of Life, back to the Door of the Sunrise and the Doors of Praise and of Wonder, ending probably at the Door of the Salutation of Majesty where he saw the statue of Marduk, and the Door of Splendour where he kissed the feet of Sarpanit.

Although when Herodotus visited Babylon the cult was in

full decline, he describes the statue of Marduk as a great figure all of gold on a golden throne, with a golden table beside it. 'I was told by the Chaldeans that to make this more than twenty-two tons of gold were used.' He also says that there were kettle-drums and incense, so that every sense must have been saturated and intoxicated in this place.

V

Occasion: Rite

When this is done, and after the second meal of the late afternoon, the urigallu-*priest of the temple Ekua shall recite to the god Bel the* Enuma elish.

The Babylonian New Year festival was held at the time of the spring equinox, in the month Nisan which is our April. We have the rubric for the liturgy of the first five days of the festival. Though the text dates only from the third or second century B.C. during the Seleucid Empire, it represents the practice of the Neo-Babylonian period. Another smaller fragment has also come to light, of a commentary that purports to explain the allegorical symbolism of the liturgy as it was understood by the celebrants. It is curious reading and between the two documents one seems almost to have before one some manual of the mass or one such as N. V. Gogol's commentary on the Divine Liturgy of the Russian Orthodox Church. The uses of symbolic action, of visual metaphor and poetic and mystical interpretation are notably akin.

New Year festivals of one sort or another belong to the most ancient traditions of an agricultural people. In Mesopotamia under the name *akitu*, a word of unknown derivation, they are referred to in third-millennium texts. The Babylonian *akitu* was certainly celebrated in the seventeenth century when a king of Babylon issued a summons to a sheep-shearing at the *Bit Akitu*, the Festival House. The New Year was not always kept in the spring but sometimes in the autumn, or even at both seasons. The spring New Year fell immediately after the harvest at threshing time, but an autumn New Year celebrated the gathering in of the last fruits before ploughing. Between these two stretched the summer season, when Tammuz died and was mourned – the parched 'dead season' of a hot country. The spring equinox was, on the whole, a moment of thankfulness and of hope tempered with foreboding. There are traces of an older Sumerian New Year in liturgies praising Ninurta or Ningirsu, who was the hero of the battle against the huge bird-winged power of the thunderstorm and the cyclone, Imdugud or Zu; while parts of the Babylonian liturgy are still in the Sumerian language which, like Latin, remained a long time sacred and embalmed. The eleven-day festival at Babylon began on the first day of the month and there were ceremonies in which fire, water, eating and drinking, sacrifice, supplication and praise all had their part, with solemn processions, concourse and vigil. Most of the ceremonies were in the early morning and in the evening, for already in Mesopotamia in April it is hot at midday and gods, like priests and people, take the siesta.

It is not known what happened on this first day, but on the second day, two hours before sunrise, the priest of Marduk got up and bathed in the water of the Euphrates. Each day begins with the same ritual washing, but the hour of rising gets progressively earlier, until on the fifth day the priest rises four hours before dawn. After robing he spreads a cloth in front of Marduk, probably for the elaborate ritual of the god's meal, the same that is mocked by Daniel in the Apocrypha *Bel and the Dragon*, when 'Daniel laughed, and said, "O King, be not deceived: for this is but clay within, and brass without, and did never eat or drink anything."' The priest chants a prayer alone in the closed sanctuary in the presence of the god, the first of many hymns which accord so well with the language of *The Babylonian Creation* that they could be transposed thence. There are parts of the liturgy that are between priest and god alone, called 'mysteries of the temple *Esagila*'; but after this hymn the doors of the sanctuary are opened and the whole company of priests and choristers enters to continue the liturgy 'in the traditional manner'. This opening of the doors corresponds liturgically to the opening of the 'Royal Gates' in the Orthodox liturgy today.

After the usual early morning ceremonies, on the third day 'when it is three hours after sunrise', a goldsmith and a wood-carver are called. From the temple treasury they are given cedar wood, tamarisk, gold and precious gems in order to make two statues for use in the ritual of the sixth day. The instructions are exact and specify material, size (seven fingers high) and form. Both are male figures; one, of tamarisk plated with gold and standing on a gold and jewelled plinth, holds in his hand a viper carved from cedar wood. The second figure holds a scorpion. These must represent two of Tiamat's monsters, the *bashmu*-viper and the scorpion–man. The rôle of the two figures is to have their heads struck off on the sixth day in front of the statue of Nabu, Marduk's son, when he has come from Borsippa.

It is possible that the writer of Isaiah xliv, 12–13 had this very ceremony in mind when he uttered his polemic against images. The time was just after Cyrus had taken Babylon and immediately before the return of the Jews from exile, when they must in fact have been perfectly familiar with Babylonian temple ceremonial.

The smith with the tongues worketh in the coals and fashioneth with hammers, and worketh it with the strength of his arms: yea, he is hungry and his strength faileth: he drinketh no water and is faint.

The carpenter stretcheth out his rule: he marketh it out with a line: he fitteth it with planes, and he marketh it with the compass, and maketh it out after the figure of a man according to the beauty of a man, that it remain in the house.

The translators of the Jerusalem Bible note that there may be a reference here to ritual fasting until the completion of the sacred work, and this would be in keeping with Babylonian ideas.

There is an impression of increasing solemnity and excitement with the passing of each day of the festival. On the morning of the fourth day 'three and one third hours of the night remaining' the priest, after washing, chants a great paean of praise in front of Marduk, in which the god is called on in words identical with those of *The Babylonian Creation*, as one who 'measures the sea, cultivates the fields ...' and so on. After certain other preliminary offices the priest goes out into the court in the centre of the temple where the night sky is paling towards dawn, and facing north he blesses the temple, singing the chant 'The Hymn of the Canal Star'. This was Dilgan or Cetus, the star identified with Babylon, which would be rising heliacally at the spring equinox. Then he opens the doors of the sanctuary for the other priests and choristers to go in and perform their traditional rites, make their offerings and sing the chants. This ends the morning ritual, for the text continues,

After the second meal of the late afternoon [meaning after the second evening sacrifice], the tiara of the god Anu and the resting-place of Enlil shall be covered, [and] the *urigallu*-priest of the temple Ekua [Marduk's chamber] shall recite, [while lifting his hand] to the god Bel the [composition entitled] *Enuma elish*.

The dramatic crisis of the festival is still ahead and the purpose of this recitation is uncertain, but it was probably felt to have been a means of giving strength to Marduk in his coming ordeal, like the cosmogonies and myths so often recited at the beginning of charms of healing.

This is the scene that we should hold in front of our eyes when reading *The Babylonian Creation*. The priest stands facing the statue of the god in the long hall; on either side, to right and left, there are recesses thirty foot deep, dark unless torches have been lit, which would catch the glimmer of gold from the roof and the blue-black sheen of lapis lazuli. Behind him the evening sky grows dark. The pale light from the door in the antechamber would hardly reach the sanctuary, even if both doors were open. There may have been other gold-covered figures beside that of Marduk in the close darkness. Then the priest begins the chant in a voice that very likely can be heard still in synagogues and mosques of the present-day East. It would have taken him well over an hour to get through the whole poem and by the end the sky above the courtyard will have become black, for this was the last act of the fourth day and now

> The Babylonian starlight brought
> a fabulous formless darkness in

The text of the commentary that we have been using takes us no farther than the fifth day. The liturgy of this day begins with a Sumerian hymn and a prayer to Beltiya that echoes the astronomical order of the fifth Tablet of Creation. The temple is purified with much censing and the beating of kettle-drums; torches are carried in procession and Nabu's chapel made ready for his arrival in the evening. The doors are smeared with sweet cedar resin, while cyprus and other aromatic ingredients are placed on a silver censer. Herodotus was told that two and a half tons of incense were burnt every year during the festival; this may be a memory of the great days of Nebuchadnezzar and his father.

There is a form of scapegoat ritual when a ram is slaughtered, and the priest who performed the sacrifice is sent out into the wilderness, not to return till after the days of the festival are over.

These are all deeply symbolic actions and their meaning can only be guessed; but the ceremonial humiliation of the king that follows on the evening of the fifth day was known and interpreted throughout the ancient world, and lasted into medieval times. But first Nabu's chapel is veiled with the 'Golden Heaven', evidently some splendid piece of material, perhaps embroidered with stars; after which all the artisans join in singing a hymn at the top of their voices, and Nabu arrives in his sacred boat. The king does not seem to have played any part in the festival up to this point, but from now on he is essential to its proper conduct. He stands robed in the antechamber of Marduk, holding the insignia of royalty: sceptre, sword and circle. The priest of Marduk takes them from him and carries them into the sanctuary where he puts them down on a chair (a throne?) in front of the god. He goes back to the king in the antechamber, strikes his cheek, then leads him into the god's presence and throws him roughly to the ground. There the bruised and humbled king says a prayer of supplication and self-justification: 'I did not sin, Lord of the countries of the world . . .' This done, the priest reassures the king, returns to him the sceptre, circle and sword, and strikes his cheek a second time. This is for a sign: if tears come it means the god is pleased, but if no tears come he is angry and enemies will rise up and bring disaster on the king.

The king is now at the centre of the festival, taking 'the hands of the god', introducing gods to the assembly, leading the procession that conducts all the gods to the Festival House, outside the gates, and back again. So important is this that if the king is not present in Babylon at the time of the festival there can be no procession. The document known as the *Nabonidas Chronicle* states that 'the king did not go to Babylon,

49

Marduk did not go forth, the *akitu* [festival] lapsed', with all that this means in loss of 'virtue', of uncertainty and peril.

There is a text which sets out to explain the occult mythological significance beyond the visible sign of the ritual. Unfortunately only fragments survive and they are difficult to read. They give an interpretation of the last act of this fifth day, which takes place at sunset. Forty reeds are tied together, placed in a pit in the great court with honey, cream and oil, a white bull is led in, and the pit set alight by the king with a burning reed; while king and priest together recite a prayer to 'the Divine Bull', 'the brilliant light that lights the darkness ...' which means Marduk, and may once, centuries before, have been identified with the constellation Taurus. The commentary states that the casting into the pit represents the enemy cast into the abyss. The forty reeds represent the monsters of chaos, and the king acts in the character of Marduk 'in his youth'. Later, when a sheep is put on the fire, this represents Kingu, who is killed, and when the king breaks a vessel it is the binding [?] of Tiamat.

Here the main commentary leaves us, and the action of the next six days can only be guessed from fragments and allusions. We know that on the eighth day the gods, already assembled from their different cities, met in synod in the *Ubshukinna* chamber for the first 'Settling of Destinies', which probably corresponds to that described on the third and fourth Tablets of Creation (in so far as the action of the poem runs parallel to that of the festival; see p. 20). This was when Marduk made his bargain with the gods and was enthroned and armed. On the tenth day all the gods were summoned out to the *Bit Akitu* and the statues, led by the king, passed down the street of the procession, under the Ishtar Gate, into boats for a short stretch on the canal and so disappeared into the temple house. What happened there is uncertain. Marduk's statue was evidently placed on a dais; there were sacrifices of sheep, cattle, fish and birds, sweet wine and watered wine; and there was a banquet. In the Assyrian version of the festival the combat of the king, impersonating the god, with Tiamat took place now in the Festival House, which was called the 'house of glad music', but the battle does not seem to have been re-enacted at Babylon.

On the eleventh day the procession returned to the temple of Marduk, the *Esagila*, and a sacred marriage may have been celebrated. There was certainly a second synod in the *Ubshukinna*, corresponding this time to that of Tablet Six, when the divine hierarchies were established and the supremacy of Marduk ratified. This was the climax of the whole festival, the instant when the eternity of the gods and the twelvemonth cycle of mankind were united, the law of the universe renewed and the sovereignty made legitimate: the king to rule as Marduk's servant until at the next New Year all had to be done again. The annual regeneration of the cosmos belongs to most systems of cyclical time, but there is here a dual conception. Linear historical time was understood as operating on the political plane of king-lists, genealogies, campaigns and battles; while on the social and natural plane time might run in ever-recurring cycles.

An odd sidelight on the interlocking of history and mythology comes from a text found at the Assyrian capital Ashur. It is a liturgy and rubric known as the 'Death and Resurrection of Bel–Marduk'. For a long time this was thought to be part of the Babylonian New Year liturgy, although its atmosphere was quite different. It shows a suffering and imprisoned Marduk, wailing women, a search, wild horses, frenzied running crowds and ceremonies at a tomb, a chariot and horses 'sent out recklessly to the house of sacrifice speeding headlong without a driver ...' and a chanting of *The Babylonian Creation*, *Enuma elish*, when the celebrant cried, 'What was the Lord's [Bel's] sin?' The mood and the symbolism are closer to those of the Tammuz liturgies, to parts of the Canaanite myth of Baal, and of the Cretan Zeus and other dying vegetation gods, than to the triumphant rejoicings of the Babylonian New Year. However it is thought now that this text had the purpose almost of a political tract, a piece of propaganda that would justify the destruction of Babylon by Sennacherib in 689 B.C. when the statue of Marduk was carried off to the Assyrian capital. By slighting the great god of the Babylonians and showing him a prisoner in the Underworld, crying out for rescue, his prestige is reduced and his priests and followers deprived of their power and boast.

If this is so, it is still not necessarily the whole truth; as so often the political expedient would hardly have been thought of without some excuse in the thought and temper of the people. The Canaanite *Epic of Baal*, the text of which was found at Ras Shamra, the ancient city of Ugarit on the Mediterranean coast opposite Cyprus, combines, after a fashion, both rituals. It has at the start the victory of Baal, in the rôle of Marduk, over the waters (a god not a goddess), his enthronement and the building of his 'house' or heavenly temple; but thereafter in the second part of the myth there is a reversal: Baal dies and descends to the world of Mot, who is Death, until he is rescued by a goddess. It is not safe to make too close connections between the semitic peoples of Syria and of Mesopotamia, but some relationship there was; and popular beliefs keep their traditional pattern, and continue to run parallel more than state religions. Death, in the Babylonian poem, has not a distinct personality like Ugaritic Mot; Lugalugga, 'King Death', is a title of Marduk himself. It is Kingu, the defeated enemy, who passes into the power of death or, in another possible reading, *becomes* Death.

VI

... Homer, who by saying 'Okeanos begetter of gods and mother Tethys' declared all things to be offspring of flux and motion.
Plato, Theaetetus, 152E

There was no lack of opportunity for Mesopotamian ideas to reach the Aegean, either through Mycenaean and Greek colonies like Ras Shamra in the fourteenth and thirteenth centuries, or al Mina, further north from the later ninth century; or through the Hittite Empire in central Anatolia, or later again through the Phrygian and Lydian kingdoms; but the extent and nature of the contacts is a matter of high controversy. The mythological cosmogonies of the poets, and the first of the philosophical cosmogonies from the Ionian Greek cities in Asia Minor, contain extraordinary similarities. Much of this is too diffused and too generalized to require any direct borrowing or imitation, but some points seem so close that any other explanation would be difficult. There are, also, the persistent traditions of oriental and 'Phoenician' secret books and teaching, which are said to have inspired the earliest Ionian philosophers.

If Homer says the universe began with a marriage between male and female waters – Ocean and Tethys – and if he also knew of the abyss, the pit of Tartaros, that dark place, as far below the earth as heaven is above it (*Iliad* viii, 13–16), this sounds remarkably familiar. But the Greeks, like the Sumerian and Akkadian inhabitants of Mesopotamia, knew of other cosmogonies and other beginnings: from night, or from a union of sky and earth, Hesiod's 'wide Ouranos and Gē, and the gods who were born to these in turn ...' The *Theogony* is a hymn, like *The Babylonian Creation*; and Hesiod's hymn was inspired by the singing of the muses to celebrate Zeus above all the other gods; while the Babylonian hymn celebrates Marduk and is sung by all the other gods. F. M. Cornford described a hymn as 'in essence an incantation, inviting the presence of a god at the sacrifice and enhancing the efficacy of the ritual. Its effectiveness is increased by a recital of the history of the god and his exploits.'[8] This fits the Babylonian as well as Hesiod's poem, if Cornford's analysis of the latter is right. He sees the *Theogony* as, in the main, a 'life-story of Zeus' in seven episodes, preceded by a short cosmogony; but although Hesiod's cosmogony has not much in common with the Babylonian there is a Sumerian myth of the marriage of An and Ki which, like Hesiod's marriage of Ouranos and Ge, was not the beginning of all things (*Theogony*, 45–6). Nor is Hesiod's Chaos, the Great Gap, at all the same as Apsu, the watery abyss. *The Babylonian Creation* has monsters but no animals, and there is no marriage of Marduk; but in the New Year festival there probably was a sacred marriage between Marduk and Sarpanit. Apart from these things omitted, the two scenarios match; and so indeed would that of Canaanite Baal. In isolating Hesiod's 'Hymn to Zeus' Cornford has had to throw out the whole Prometheus myth, and the 'Anatolian' story of Kronos and the birth of Zeus, which are embedded in Hesiod's hymn, and this leaves 'the scattered débris of a single creation myth ... the myth itself is a reflection of the New Year ritual'. He also believed that the cosmogonical myth was not of Hellenic origin, but derived by the Greeks from oriental sources current in Crete and Asia Minor.

There are, of course, great and revealing differences. The rôle of Earth is closer in the Greek and the Sumerian, and the threefold division of the universe between Zeus, Poseidon and Hades, presupposed by the *Iliad* and by Pherecydes in the sixth

8. *Principium Sapientiae*, 1952, p. 192.

century,[9] also has a Sumerian counterpart as already quoted (p. 33 above). Tiamat's monsters did not throw stones; but the mysterious 'small ones' and 'great ones' hurled against Enki in the Sumerian cosmogony may be cousins of Zeus's rock-hurling giants. Typhoeus, with his hundred serpent heads flashing fire, is more like a volcano in eruption than a sea monster; but just such a monster is the *bashmu*, first of Tiamat's horde. Some think that the concept of Ocean as a great river that runs around the earth was taken into Greek thought from one of the river civilizations, Egypt or Mesopotamia, where a vision of the earth emerging out of the waters has more physical justification than it would in mountainous stony Greece or Anatolia; but if the word *okeanos* is really related to an Akkadian word meaning circle, *uginna*, this sounds like the same idea as Anshar and Kishar, the great circling horizon of sky and earth.[10] There is one point at which Greek *chaos*, the gulf or chasm full of storms, does coincide with Apsu, the abyss, and that is in vastness of scale and also (implicitly) its boundaries; for the Assyriologist E. A. Speiser writes that *Apsu* also has this dual meaning of almost limitless size and yet of limitation, the last bounds. There is a tantalizing hint, found in Eusebius, historian, and bishop of Caesarea in Palestine at the beginning of the fourth century, which is usually rejected as unreliable, but which reproduces much earlier matter: it is of a Phoenician cosmogony that began in a state of boundless gloom, with air and wind, which, after mingling with something akin to itself (its ἀρχαί) produced slime from which arose the rest of creation. It is possible that this rejected 'slime' was the same as the sediments Lahmu and Lahamu, the first consequence of the

9. 'Zas and Chronos always existed and Chthonie; and Chthonie got the name of Gē, since Zas gave her Gē as a present or prerogative.' (Kirk and Raven, *The Presocratic Philosophers*, 1966, pp. 54–5.)

10. On Pherecydes, see Kirk and Raven, *The Presocratic Philosophers*, 1966, pp. 48, 62.

mingling of Tiamat and Apsu. Orphic origins also postulated water, from which came slime, and from the slime the dragon that laid the egg that divided into the two half-spheres of Sky and Earth.

Writing on early *Greek Epic Poetry*, George Huxley quotes the fragment of Euripides' *Melanippe the Wise* and other lost cycles of epic which begin with the union of sky and earth, and he concludes that Greek 'poets had to choose between the primeval parentage of Ouranos and Earth in one system or Okeanos and Tethys in another'. It is the same choice that the people of Mesopotamia had; and the poet of *The Babylonian Creation* chose the second.[11]

The Ionian philosopher, physicist and astronomer, Thales, is reputed to have held that the earth floated on the waters like a log, and such a belief in a watery beginning of the world was probably not just a rationalization of the Homeric Tethys and Okeanos, but came from further east. Whether this traffic in ideas should be carried back to the Bronze Age, or whether it belongs to the 'orientalizing' period of much more recent date, or even to the unknown explorations of the dark age between, cannot be said. The confusion of the evidence may be due to the many layers of contact, divided in time and different in nature. Among the points that favour some early connection are the undoubted parallels with the Ugaritic mythology of northern Syria among which is the (late) tradition that the battle between Zeus and Typhoeus was fought on Mount Casius, the high seat of Ugaritic Baal near Ras Shamra. There is also a curious collection of Mesopotamian Cassite seals found in Late Bronze-Age Thebes in Boeotia. The Cassites were a foreign dynasty that invaded and ruled Babylonia from the beginning of the sixteenth to the middle of the thirteenth century B.C. It was during the Cassite domination that the authority of Marduk increased so dramatically in Babylon,

11. See G. L. Huxley, *Greek Epic Poetry*, 1969, pp. 21, 30.

while the social upheavals of the times helped to undermine the authority of older Sumerian gods. Babylonian stories certainly travelled west in the fourteenth century, for a text of the *Adapa* myth was found at Tell el Amarna in Egypt (1379–1362; see p. 167), while a Cassite seal and much Mycenean pottery have been dug up in a temple of oriental plan at Amman.

Thales, Anaximander and their successors, from around 600 B.C. onwards, transformed such oriental ideas as did penetrate to the Aegean into rational inquiry in the spirit of science and a new philosophy, until they lost all likeness to their originals; and after Thales the evanescent mythological vision changes almost incredibly fast to the bony framework of an intelligible universe in which, as Henri Frankfort wrote in *The Intellectual Adventure of Ancient Man*, 'reason is acknowledged as the highest arbiter . . . [it is] this tacit or outspoken appeal to reason, no less than the independence from the "prescriptive sanctities of religion", which places early Greek philosophy in the sharpest contrast with the thought of the ancient Near East'. Thales of Miletus was probably of mixed Greek and Anatolian heredity and he was reported, not improbably, to have visited Egypt. Tradition had it that his most renowned feat was his prediction of the eclipse of 585 B.C. which interrupted the war between the Medes and Lydians in Anatolia. Babylonian astronomers had been predicting eclipses, to the year, for at least a century, so establishing a cycle of solstices within which they could be expected. In Babylon it was the priests of Marduk who were the masters of a learning in which astronomy and astrology, religion and science, mingled.

Although these new intellectual horizons, with new powers of abstraction beyond the capacity of any earlier age, had emerged in the little towns of the Ionian Greeks in Asia Minor, still quaint outmoded ideas would keep cropping up, in a chorus of Aristophanes' *Birds*, or a tale told in Euripides, as well as within the constant, potent aura of the Mystery religions. Eleusis and the Orphics kept much of the old religions alive, but rather as a kind of psychology than as a creed or body of doctrine. These were, to borrow biological terms, live mutations rather than dead fossils. Both fossil and mutant exist side by side in the writings of Berossus, a priest of Bel–Marduk in Babylon. He might just, as a young boy, have seen Alexander, for he lived at the turn of the third century, two hundred years after the desecration of Marduk's temple by Xerxes. Round about 275 B.C. he wrote in Greek a history of Babylonia, in which he drew on much older material. Only fragments have come down to us from the first book of his history, but one of these describes the original state of the universe as of darkness and water, ruled by Omorka, which is a title of Tiamat. She is the mother of monsters which are said to be the same as the dragons and great beasts shown on the gates and walls of Babylon. This must represent what people thought in his own day. He also tells of the separation of Omorka–Tiamat by Bel into the two halves of sky and earth, and says that he 'reduced the universe to order', and made man and animals from the blood of a god who was commanded to cut off his own head, and that the other gods mixed the blood with earth so that 'men are rational and partake of divine understanding'. The cutting off of his own head by the god is not heard of anywhere else in the cuneiform texts, but mixing blood and earth and its consequence, may come from the *Atrahasis Epic*. The formation of animals, as well as man, from the blood of the slain god is peculiar to Berossus. His Bel was a source of light so insufferable that it caused the monsters to perish, and mankind was created to people and cultivate the desolate earth.

We owe the survival of this fragment to an unusual chance, for Eusebius quoted it in a chronicle of world history, again for the most part lost, and from him it passed into the writings of George Synkellos, a monk who lived in Constantinople in the eighth century A.D.; Eusebius identified Bel with Zeus.

A second version of *The Babylonian Creation* was known to the world before the translation of cuneiform through the writings of Damascius, a late Neo-Platonist philosopher who composed, around A.D. 480, a treatise on *Difficulties and Solutions of First Principles*. In this he gave a brief, but remarkably accurate, summary of the opening of *The Babylonian Creation*, in which Mummu appears as Moymis or Mumis, and Apsu and Tiamat as Apason and Tauthe. Tiamat bears generations of gods, among whom Lahmu and Lahamu are easily recognized, also Anshar and Kishar, Anu, Enlil and Ea; these three last are the children of Anshar and Kishar, whereas in our poem Ea is the son of Anu, and Enlil has no parentage, so Damascius is probably using a different equally authentic tradition. Aos and Dauthe (Ea and Damkina) appear as parents of Bel who is the 'fabricator of the world', the demiurge.

Damascius too must have used several cuneiform sources, one of which was *Enuma elish*; while Eusebius only chose to preserve those parts of Berossus that he thought would appeal to the curiosity and love of marvels of his age; so his account has the description of monsters such as might be at home in medieval bestiaries. More interesting than the accuracy or error of the details, is the *fact* of this fragile link between Nebuchadnezzar's Babylon and (through George Synkellos) the Byzantium of the Ikonoklasts. But after all it was never so far from 'Babylon, that pearl of kingdoms' to 'the holy city of Byzantium', for poetically was not Babylon Byzantium's Byzantium?

VII

In the beginning . . .

There is one last topic, which perhaps should have been the first, and which it would be craven to ignore; but it is of such complexity that a version of ancient texts, the main purpose of which is to entertain, can only allude to it superficially: I mean the relationship between our poem and ancient Hebrew writings. If Thales 'turned the Babylonian creation myth into natural philosophy', in Judea 'profound religious minds appropriated . . . and changed it into history by incorporating it, as the first part, in God's redemptive historical revelation'.[12] This remark of a biblical scholar probably puts it too strongly but, from the first publication of *Enuma elish* in 1876, with the title *The Chaldean Account of Genesis*, it has constantly been set beside the opening chapters of the Bible. His edition of *Enuma elish* Alexander Heidel calls *The Babylonian Genesis*, but in a chapter on 'Old Testament Parallels' he underlines the real differences that exist within language that is often very similar; while another Assyriologist writes that 'it seems very probable that the epic [*Enuma elish*] has no connection of any kind, or at any point, with Genesis'.[13] Between opinions so opposite and so categoric obviously no reconciliation is possible.

If we compare the first words of both accounts, the 'when' of *Enuma elish*, with 'In the beginning . . .', then the Akkadian word means 'on the day that' . . . the day, any day that it happened, and is properly translated as 'when'. It corresponds

12. T. Boman, *Hebrew Thought Compared with Greek*, 1954, 1960, p. 180.

13. Kinnier Wilson in *Documents from Old Testament Times*, ed. D. W. Thomas, 1958, pp. 3 f.

(as Heidel points out) to Hebrew *beyōm*; but the *berēshīth* of the priestly account of creation is no cosmogonic event taking place outside time, both reversible and repeatable; quite the contrary, it is the beginning of history. In the Babylonian poem there is, strictly speaking, no creation at all. Matter is eternal, Tiamat and Apsu provide, from within themselves, the material of the whole universe; a universe which will evolve into ever greater complexity through processes of biological reproduction (of gods!) without any external creative act, or the need of a creator. Marduk does not 'create' the sun and moon; he gives them their occupation and sends them about their business. When he is called 'creator' of mankind, this is not creation *ex nihilo*; there would be no man without the sacrifice of Kingu the rebel god.

Babylonian and Hebrew (the Priestly account) are alike in the conception of an immense primeval body of water from which the earth was separated out. 'Darkness was upon the face of the deep' (Genesis i, 2a) has also been translated 'a great wind swept over the deep'. Akkadian *Tiamat* and Hebrew *tehōm*, usually translated 'the deep', are etymologically linked; but Tiamat is a proper name, while *tehom*, like Akkadian *tāmtu*, means any large body of water, and the two are not interchangeable. *Tehom* may actually be an older formation, but both probably go back to a common semitic parent. It is the same with many other superficial likenesses: the creation of the firmament dividing the upper and nether waters, and the existence of light, the 'glory' of Apsu taken from him by Ea, before the appearance of sun, moon and stars; with the creation of man as the last act in both programmes. A relationship of sorts is there, but of just what sort is not easy to discover, for the Hebrew account has, of course, been profoundly de-mythologized.

The dates usually proposed for the composition of Genesis run from the tenth century, for the Yahwist account, to the sixth or later for the Priestly. If in fact Genesis was 'given its original written form during the time when the Davidic empire was being established' with 'additions and supplements of later authors only intended to help bridge the gap for contemporary readers',[14] and if the world described is for the most part that of the tenth and eleventh centuries, and if Professor Lambert's date for the composition of *Enuma elish*, the later twelfth century, is also the right one; then whatever there is of likeness between the two would be due to their common dependence on the broad background of Mesopotamian religious thought with its various myths of origins, rather than to any direct borrowing of this or that expression or incident.

Israel could have got its Babylonian imagery at various times. There was the ill-defined phase of perhaps very close contact with Babylonian civilization before the Patriarchs arrived in the Land of Canaan; and there are better defined but indirect contacts through Canaanite neighbours after the Exodus from Egypt. Stories and poems could and did travel west during the fourteenth century, when Babylonian was the language of diplomacy throughout western Asia, including Syria and Palestine. The text of *Adapa*, found in the archives of the Pharaohs Amenhotep III and IV at Tell el Amarna in Egypt, has already been referred to. Travellers in the caravans that followed the ancient trade routes in the following centuries brought to Israel that 'wisdom of the peoples of the East' which Solomon set out to rival until, in the sixth century, in the calamitous years of exile under Nebuchadnezzar II, there was again cheek-by-jowl contact. This is what we have in the later prophetic books, where acquaintance with Babylon is sharp, hard, historical and turns to satire and polemic. Far more important than this or that similar detail of tradition is, to quote Professor Hooke, the fact that 'the Hebrew writers did not have to invent an order of symbolism but took what

14. B. Mazer, *Journal of Near Eastern Studies* (April 1969), p. 73.

lay ready to hand, the ancient symbols of Mesopotamia', and so put them to their own uses.

If we are, as I think we are, right in calling *The Babylonian Creation* not an epic, but a hymn of praise to Marduk, then it is not surprising to find that its language has so much less in common with the narrative of Genesis than with the poetic books of the Old Testament: Psalms, Job and parts of Isaiah, but especially with those psalms that are Enthronement Songs, Royal Songs, and Liturgical Songs celebrating Yahweh with the ritual of the New Year festival in Jerusalem. There is no sign in Genesis of the battle between chaos and cosmos, Tiamat and Marduk, but in the Psalms, in Job and in Isaiah there lurk 'shattered fragments' of the myth of conflict between Yahweh and some great monster at the beginning of the world:

> The Shades tremble beneath the earth;
>   the waters and their denizens are afraid.
> Before his eyes Sheol is bare,
>   Perdition itself is uncovered . . .
>
> With his power he calmed the Sea
>   with his wisdom struck Rahab down.
> His breath made the heaven luminous,
>   his hand transfixed the Fleeing Serpent.
> All this but skirts the way he treads,
>   a whispered echo is all that we hear of him.
> But who could comprehend the thunder of his Power?
>   (Job, xxvi, Jerusalem Bible)

Rahab is a monster of the primeval world, destroyed, it may be noted, by the same weapon with which Ea destroyed Apsu – 'wisdom'. The Fleeing Serpent is Leviathan, who appears also in the Canaanite poems from Ugarit as Lotan, the 'slippery serpent' and the 'wriggling' or 'winding' serpent, Shalyat of the Seven Heads, the hydra struck down by Baal in the fourteenth-century Baal epic.[15] For the writer of Job they are probably no more than faint rumours of a half-forgotten conflict between tremendous powers of the remote past. To us the 'whispered echo' of the next to last line may have a very modern sound recalling the background 'whisper' picked up from interstellar space, and believed by adherents of the 'Big Bang' theory of cosmic beginnings to be the last ripple of that event.

> By your power you split the sea in two,
> You smashed the heads of monsters on the waters.
> You crushed Leviathan's heads
> Leaving him for wild animals to eat,
> You opened the spring, the torrent,
> You dried up inexhaustible rivers.
> You are master of day and night,
> You instituted light and sun,
> You fixed the boundaries of the world,
> You created summer and winter.
>
> (Psalm lxxiv; Jerusalem Bible)

The order of events – the division of the sea and shattering of Leviathan, set immediately before the institution of day and night, summer and winter – carries this vision back into the time of beginnings with the days of creation. These dragons and sea monsters may be poetical metaphors for the chief enemy of the moment, but their use as references presupposes an understanding of the thing referred to. They may be demythologized into crocodiles and snakes, or kings of Egypt and Assyria; but it does not follow that they meant nothing more than that to the authors of Job or of Psalm lxxiv. At other times, as in Psalm xxx, Yahweh triumphing over the destruction of Assyria could as well be Marduk setting out against Tiamat.

15. G. R. Driver, *Canaanite Myths and Legends*, 1956; and W. Albright, *Yahveh and the Gods of Canaan*, 1968, p. 175.

... his nostrils burn, thick clouds arise,
his lips are boiling over with rage,
　his tongue is like a devouring fire,
and his breath is like an overflowing stream ...
(trans. Michelet, Mowinkel, Messel)

Scattered through the poetic books of the Bible these images deepen the terror and mystery that belong to an earlier world behind the limit of memory.

This introduction began with the great Babylonian paradox: 'Babylon the glory of kingdoms, the beauty of the Chaldees' excellency, shall be as when God overthrew Sodom and Gomorrah'; it is the paradox of a beautiful creation that is forever doomed. There is one passage in Isaiah in which this feeling has its most mysterious expression. It is a passage that has moved and inspired many poets, and quite lately light has broken on it from a rather unexpected quarter:

How art thou fallen from heaven O Lucifer, son of the morning

The poet here is specifically composing a satire on the death of a tyrant, *the* tyrant Nebuchadnezzar II. The Jerusalem Bible has:

The day Yahweh gives you rest after your suffering and torment and the grim servitude to which you were forcibly enslaved, you are to recite this satire on the king of Babylon.

The Lucifer passage is given:

How did you come to fall from the heavens
Daystar, son of Dawn?
You who enslaved the nations?
You who used to think to yourself
'I will climb up to the heavens;
And higher than the stars of God [El]
I will set my throne.
I will sit on the Mount of Assembly
In the recesses of the north [Saphon].

I will climb to the top of the thunderclouds,
I will rival the Most High ['Elyōn].'
What! Now you have fallen to Sheol
To the very bottom of the abyss.

Daystar, son of Dawn, is *Hēlel ben Shahar* in Hebrew, *Eōs-phoros* in the Septuagint, *Lucifer* in the Vulgate; understood in all as the planet Venus, conspicuous in the morning sky but fading in the sun's light; fading but not falling. What has this starry allegory to do with the destruction of a hated but very human tyrant, and, still more, what with Lucifer, the prince of the fallen angels, Milton's Satan, the devil? This whole passage is now thought to be a quotation from an old Canaanite myth. Its language is that of the Canaanite poems. Shahar is also the Ugaritic 'Dawn' and Helel means the 'bright shiner'. El, translated as 'God', is also the Canaanite father of all the gods; the word given as 'recesses of the north', Saphon, is Mount Casius, the highest mountain in northern Syria, just visible from Ras Shamra but also, like the Greek Olympos, the ethereal assembly of the gods in heaven. There are some uncertainties in the argument, but the mythology behind this poem probably concerns Baal, whose name, like Bēl and Adonis, means Lord. Baal was a beneficent god who brought the rains and conquered Leviathan and the Flood. Towards the end of his epic he is no longer on earth but in the underworld and subject to Mot, its ruler. A younger god called ʿAthtar the Proud, or Presumptuous, attempts to sit on his throne and take his place, but his feet do not reach the footstool, nor his head the top (that is the summit of the holy mountain).

He came down, Athtar the Proud, came down.

He left Saphon apparently to rule 'on god's earth'. After a gap in the text Baal returns and throws down 'the sons of Athirat', of whom Athtar was perhaps the favourite. This crucial passage is, in G. R. Driver's translation,

66

Baal seized the sons of Athirat:
he smote [them, though] mighty, with a sword,
smote [them, though] resplendent with a mace;
[and] Mot did gape open [that] they might go right
  into the earth
[Athtar] came down from the throne of his kingdom,
from [the resting place], from the seat of his dominion.

Several words are uncertain, including the naming of Athtar,
but if the rendering is accepted this was a fall indeed, like the
fall of the Titans, for Mot is death and whoever enters his jaws
enters Sheol, Hades, hell.[16] Athtar is of the same lineage as,
though not the son of, Shahar, the Dawn, and his name is
linked with the Morning Star in southern Arabia, in Moab, and
in Phoenicia as ʿAshtar and ʿAshtor, and in its Aramaic form
ʿAttar-Shamayin, which is translated Morning Star of Heaven.
It has been suggested that the same myth lies behind the figure
of Phaethon. In Hesiod he is the son of the Dawn and his name,
like Hēlel, means 'brilliant one', 'bright shiner'. But Greek
mythology knew another Phaethon, a son of the sun who
tried presumptuously to usurp his father's place and, driving
his chariot too near the earth, was destroyed by a thunderbolt
which sent him hurtling from the skies. This Phaethon, who
appears first in Euripides, was, like Athtar the Proud, the
victim of *hubris*, the unpardonable sin. Whether or not Greeks,
Syrians and Israelites drew on the same myth (and an inde-
pendent invention is quite possible) we certainly have in the
Ugaritic texts a fragment of mythology concerned with the

16. G. R. Driver, *Canaanite Myths and Legends*, 1956, p. 113; Driver,
however, takes Athtar for a god of springs, wells and irrigation. Another
translation has, 'Mot is vanquished, reaches earth.' The argument para-
phrased here is taken from W. Albright, *Yahveh and the Gods of Canaan*,
1968, *Archaeology and the Religion of Israel*, 1946, 1953, pp. 83 f.; John
Gray, *The Canaanites*, 1964, pp. 125 f. and 'The Legacy of Canaan',
1965, p. 66; P. Grelot in *Revue de l'Histoire des Religions* 1956, pp. 18-48
which links it with Phaethon and Greek mythology.

theme of usurpation and the fall of gods. The fate of Athtar makes fair comparison for the allegory of Isaiah and the doom of Babylon and thence as *one* source of the Christian (and late pagan) allegory of the pride and presumption of Lucifer and his fall, with the long rolls of its thunder still heard in Western poetry to the present day.

If all this is accepted it is still puzzling why the king of Babylon, the subject of Isaiah's taunt and a mere man, should be linked to this bright star and fallen god. The language is too exaggerated, even as oriental hyperbole; for what mortal claims to climb 'higher than the stars of God' and to rival ''Elyōn, the Most High'? If there is an explanation it may lie in the relationship of the king of Babylon to his god. At the New Year festival the king 'takes the hands of Marduk' and leads him out, he becomes his regent on earth: as Marduk in heaven so Nebuchadnezzar in Babylon. If the subject were Marduk himself this language would be appropriate, and all would be explained. The difficulty here is that none of the titles of Marduk connects him with Venus, the Morning Star, which was the goddess Ishtar's planet. But the title with which his father greets him when he first sees his beauty is: 'My son, my son, son of the sun and the heaven's sun [*mar shamshu shamshu sha shamē*].' Marduk is another 'bright shiner', like Helel, like Phaethon, like Lucifer. Whether or not there is any link with *Baʿal-shamēm* is another matter.[17] There is nothing here to suggest Marduk's wretched adversary Kingu, sacrificed to make mankind, except that, like Athtar, he was a usurper.

The Ugaritic *Baal* was written down in the first half of the fourteenth century B.C.; *The Babylonian Creation*, with its version of the war in heaven, probably in the twelfth century; the poet of Isaiah xiv was writing in the sixth. Milton finished Paradise Lost in 1663; he knew nothing of Marduk and very little about Baal, but strangely enough both the plural *Baalim*

17. Albright, op. cit., 1968, p. 198.

and Athtar's female counterpart the Phoenician *Ashtaroth* join in Milton's *Hymn on the Morning of Christ's Nativity*.

> Peor and Baalim
> Forsake their temples dim
>   With that twice-batter'd god of Palestine
> And mooned Ashtaroth
> Heaven's queen and mother both
>   Now sits not girt with tapers' holy shine.

His Lucifer was of their lineage and the myth remains true even to its central motivation, the reward of pride.

> . . . . . . what time his pride
> Had cast him out of heaven, with all his host
> Of rebel Angels; by whose aid aspiring
> To set himself in glory above his peers,
> He trusted to have equal'd the Most High
> If he opposed; and with ambitious aim
> Against the throne and monarchy of God
> Raised impious war in heaven and battel proud
> With vain attempt. Him the Almighty Power
> Hurl'd headlong flaming from the ethereal sky
> With hideous ruin and combustion down
> To bottomless perdition . . .

Of the many threads and themes that are united in Milton's poem the one just traced is possibly the oldest, and is not the least curious.

The physical universe – radiation, gravitation, electrical fields, explosions and collisions – is a man-made metaphor, not reality itself; and the conflicts of Apsu and Ea, Tiamat and Marduk, are neither more nor less than that. If an hypothesis be deemed true 'if it works', and if for us the general theory of relativity and quantum physics work, then the death and resurrection of Tammuz or Baal and the great Settling of Destinies once a year by Marduk and the assembled gods in

Babylon did truly work. The punctual rising of sun and moon and stars, and the returning seasons were positive proof of this. Our senses and capacities set our limitations; our reason can only work on them; however we dress them up with contemporary jargon, our fundamental ideas about the world remain unchanged and unchanging. We can choose today between Continuous Creation and the Big Bang, and the ancient world had the same choice. Creation of the universe *ex nihilo* by Yahweh was a cataclysmic physical event as much as any Big Bang, or series of bangs which may still be whispering round the universe; while the cyclical turnings of time, and the eternal uncreated matter of the Babylonian cosmogony, perpetually evolving into greater complexity yet liable to regress into a simpler state, has its counterpart in Continuous Creation.

Whatever the nature of the difference, whether theological or physical, it surely represents at bottom a difference of psychological, or mental, tone. We do not know the reason but it is very probable that the antinomy was there from the first beginning of man's thoughts about beginnings.

VIII

Note on Sources

This English version of *The Babylonian Creation* is based on a number of different sources, among which the most important are: for Tablets I–IV and VI–VII, S. Langdon, *The Babylonian Epic of Creation*, 1923, Akkadian (Assyrian) version and English translation; R. Labat, *Le poème babylonien de la création*, 1935, Akkadian and French translation; A. Heidel, *The Babylonian Genesis*, 2nd edn, 1951, English only; E. A. Speiser in *Ancient Near Eastern Texts Relating to the Old*

Testament, 2nd edn, 1955, the fullest English translation at present available, and the Temple Progamme for the New Year festival. For Tablet V, B. Landsberger and J. V. Kinnier Wilson, *Journal of Near Eastern Studies* 20 (1961), pp. 154–79, Akkadian and English; also extracts by Kinnier Wilson in *Documents from Old Testament Times*, ed. D. W. Thomas, 1958, and Thorkild Jacobsen in *Religions in Antiquity*, seminar edited by J. Neusner, Comparative Studies Center, Dartmouth College, U.S.A., W. G. Lambert has published the fullest cuneiform text which fills in most of the gaps in Tablet II (151 lines, partially restored, as against 129 in Speiser), *Enuma elish*, 1967.

The titles of Marduk in the Hymn of Tablets VI–VII are discussed and where possible translated by T. Böhl, *Archiv für Orientforschung*, 11 (1936), pp. 191–218; and K. Tallqvist, *Akkadische Götterepithete* (1938).

THE BABYLONIAN CREATION

I

WHEN there was no heaven,
no earth, no height, no depth, no name,
when Apsu was alone,
the sweet water, the first begetter; and Tiamat
the bitter water, and that
return to the womb, her Mummu,
when there were no gods –

When sweet and bitter
mingled together, no reed was plaited, no rushes
muddied the water,
the gods were nameless, natureless, futureless, then
from Apsu and Tiamat
in the waters gods were created, in the waters
silt precipitated,

Lahmu and Lahamu,
were named; they were not yet old,
not yet grown tall
when Anshar and Kishar overtook them both,
the lines of sky and earth
stretched where horizons meet to separate
cloud from silt.

Days on days, years
on years passed till Anu, the empty heaven,
heir and supplanter,

first-born of his father, in his own nature
    begot Nudimmud-Ea,
intellect, wisdom, wider than heaven's horizon,
    the strongest of all the kindred.

Discord broke out among the gods although they were
brothers, warring and jarring in the belly of Tiamat, heaven
shook, it reeled with the surge of the dance; Apsu could not
silence the clamour, their behaviour was bad, overbearing and
proud.

But still Tiamat lay inert till Apsu, the father of gods, bellowed
for that servant who clouds his judgement, his Mummu,
    'Dear counsellor, come with me to Tiamat.'
They have gone, and in front of Tiamat they sit down and talk
together about the young gods, their first-born children; Apsu
said,

    'Their manners revolt me, day and night without remis-
sion we suffer. My will is to destroy them, all of their kind, we
shall have peace at last and we will sleep again.'

When Tiamat heard she was stung, she writhed in lonely
desolation, her heart worked in secret passion, Tiamat said,
    'Why must we destroy the children that we made? If their
ways are troublesome, let us wait a little while.'

Then Mummu advised Apsu, and he spoke in malice,
    'Father, destroy them in full rebellion, you will have quiet
in the daytime and at night you will sleep.'

When Apsu heard, the die was cast against his children, his face
flamed with the pleasure of evil; but Mummu he embraced,
he hung on his neck, he sat him down on his knees and kissed
him.

The decision was known to all their children; confusion seized them and after, a great silence, for they were confounded.

The god who is the source of wisdom, the bright intelligence that perceives and plans, Nudimmud-Ea, saw through it, he sounded the coil of chaos, and against it devised the artifice of the universe.

He spoke the word that charmed the waters, it fell upon Apsu, he lay asleep, the sweet waters slept, Apsu slept, Mummu was overcome, Apsu lay drowned, undone.

Then Ea ripped off his flaming glory coat and took his crown, he set on himself the aureole of the king. When Ea had bound Apsu he killed him, and Mummu, the dark counsellor, he led by the nose and locked away.

Ea had defeated his enemies and trodden them down. Now that his triumph was completed, in deep peace he rested, in his holy palace Ea slept. Over the abyss, the distance, he built his house and shrine and there magnificently he lived with his wife Damkina.

In that room, at the point of decision where what is to come is predetermined, he was conceived, the most sagacious, the one from the first most absolute in action.

In the deep abyss he was conceived, MARDUK was made in the heart of the apsu, MARDUK was created in the heart of the holy apsu. Ea begot him and Damkina bore him, father and mother; he sucked the paps of goddesses, from his nurses he was fed on the terribleness that filled him.

His body was beautiful; when he raised his eyes great lights flared; his stride was majestic; he was the leader from the first.

When Ea who begot him saw him he exulted, he was radiant,

75

light-hearted, for he saw that he was perfect, and he multiplied his godhead, the one to be first and stand highest.

His limbs were immaculate, the making a fearful mystery beyond comprehension; with four eyes for limitless sight, and four ears hearing all; when his lips moved a tongue of fire burst out. Titanic limbs, standing so high he overtopped the tallest god; he was strong and he wore the glory of ten, and their lightnings played round him.

'My son, my son, son of the sun, and heaven's sun!'

Then Anu begot winds and brought them from the four quarters, to be the van and to command the ranks; and he brought the tornado, a wild surf to worry Tiamat.

But now the other gods had no rest any more, tormented by storms, they conspired in their secret hearts and brought to Tiamat the matter of their plot. To their own mother they said,

'When they killed Apsu you did not stir, you brought no help to him, your husband. Now Anu has called up from the four quarters this abomination of winds to rage in your guts, and we cannot rest for the pain;

'Remember Apsu in your heart, your husband, remember Mummu who was defeated; now you are all alone, and thrash around in desolation, and we have lost your love, our eyes ache and we long for sleep.

'Rouse up, our Mother! Pay them back and make them empty like the wind.'

Tiamat approved it, she said,

'I approve this advice: we will make monsters, and monsters and gods against gods will march into battle together.'

Together they jostle the ranks to march with Tiamat, day and night furiously they plot, the growling roaring rout, ready for battle, while the Old Hag, the first mother, mothers a new brood.

She loosed the irresistible missile, she spawned enormous serpents with cutting fangs, chock-full of venom instead of blood, snarling dragons wearing their glory like gods. (Whoever sees this thing receives the shock of death, for when they heave those bodies up they never turn them back.)

> She made the Worm
> the Dragon
> the Female Monster
> the Great Lion
> the Mad Dog
> the Man Scorpion
> the Howling Storm
> Kulili
> Kusariqu

There was no pity in their weapons, they did not flinch from battle for her law was binding, irrevocable.

Eleven such monsters she made, but she took from among the gods the clumsy labourer

KINGU

one of the first generation to be her Captain, War-leader, Assembly-leader, ordering the supplies, leading the van to battle

SUPREME COMMANDER OF THE WARS

All this she gave him when she raised their Company, she said,

'Now it is in your hands, my spell will hold them bound, they must obey my will. You are supreme, my one husband, your word will hold the rebel horde.'

She gave him the Tables of Fate and fastened them on to his breast,

'Now and for evermore your word is irrevocable, your judgements will last! They will quench the fire and the swinging mace will fail of its power.'

When Kingu had received the authority, that belonged before to Anu, in their several natures they confirmed the brood of monsters.

II

When her labour of creation was ended, against her children Tiamat began preparations of war. This was the evil she did to requite Apsu, this was the evil news that came to Ea.

When he had learned how matters lay he was stunned, he sat in black silence till rage had worked itself out; then he remembered the gods before him. He went to Anshar, his father's father, and told him how Tiamat plotted,

'She loathes us, father, our mother Tiamat has raised up that Company, she rages in turbulence and all have joined her, all those gods whom you begot,

'Together they jostle the ranks to march with Tiamat, day and night furiously they plot, the growling roaring rout, ready for battle, while the Old Hag, the first mother, mothers a new brood.

'She has loosed the irresistible missile, spawned enormous serpents with cutting fangs, chock-full of venom instead of blood, snarling dragons wearing their glory like gods. (Whoever sees this thing receives the shock of death, for when they heave those bodies up they never turn them back.)

'She has made the Worm,
the Dragon
the Female Monster
the Great Lion
the Mad Dog
the Man Scorpion
the Howling Storm
Kulili
Kusariqu

'There is no pity in their weapons, they do not flinch from battle for her law is binding, irrevocable.

'Eleven such monsters she has made but she took from among the gods the clumsy labourer

KINGU

one of the first generation to be her Captain, War-leader, Assembly-leader, ordering the supplies, leading the van to battle

SUPREME COMMANDER OF THE WARS

All this she gave him when she raised their Company, she has said,

'"Now it is in your hands, my spell will hold them bound, they must obey my will. You are supreme, my one husband, your word will hold the rebel horde."'

She has given to him the Tables of Fate and fastened them on to his breast,
'"Now and for evermore your word is irrevocable, your

judgements will last! They will quench the fire and the swinging mace will fail of its power."

So Kingu has received the authority that belonged before to Anu, they have confirmed in their several natures the brood of monsters.'

When Anshar heard how the Tiamat-tempest was rising he struck his groin, bit his lip, restless, gloomy and sick at heart, he covered his mouth to stifle his groans.

At last he spoke, urging Ea on to the fight,
  'Once you made a snare of words, now go and try it out. You killed Mummu, killed Apsu; kill Kingu who marches in front of Tiamat!'

The sagacious counsellor of all the gods, Nudimmud-Ea, answered Anshar . . .

[break of eight lines partially reconstructed]

  'I will meet Tiamat and calm her spirit, when her heart brims over she will hear my words, and if not mine then yours may appease the waters.'

Nudimmud took the short road, went the direct way to Tiamat; but when he saw her whole strategy he could not face her, but he came back cringing.

So Anshar called his son Anu,
  'This is the true hero, an irresistible onslaught, a strong god. Go, and face Tiamat, and calm her spirit; when her heart brims over she will listen to you, but if she remains unreconciled my word may appease the waters.'

Anu obeyed his father's orders, he took the short road, went the direct way to Tiamat; but when he had come so close that he saw her whole strategy, he could not face her, he came back cringing to his father Anshar.

He spoke as though he saw Tiamat still,
    'My hands are too weak, I cannot conquer her.'

Anshar was dumb; he stared at the ground and his hair stood on end. He shook his head at Ea, all the Anunnaki, the host of gods gathered into that place tongue-tied; they sat with mouths shut for they thought,

    'What other god can make war on Tiamat? No one else can face her and come back.'

Then the Lord, the father of gods, Anshar rose to his feet majestically. Having considered everything he spoke to the Anunnaki,
    'Which one of us is impetuous in battle? The hero Marduk! Only he is strong enough to avenge us.'

Then Ea called Marduk into a secret place and gave him subtle advice out of his deep mind,
    'You are the dear son who warms my heart, Marduk. When you see Anshar go straight to him as you would go into battle. Stand up when you speak, and when he sees you he will grow calm.'

Lord Marduk exulted, he strode forward and stood facing Anshar. When Anshar saw him his heart swelled with joy, he kissed him on the lips and shook off despair.

    'Anshar, break your silence, let your words ring out for I will accomplish what you long for most in your heart. What hero has forced the battle on you? Only a female thing, only Tiamat flies at you with all her contrivance. You shall soon straddle Tiamat's neck.'

    'My son, my wise son, confuse Tiamat with charged

words, go quickly now, the storm is your chariot, they will never deflect you from Tiamat, but having done with her, then return.'

The Lord exulted, with racing spirits he said to the father of gods,

'Creator of the gods who decides their destiny, if I must be your avenger, defeating Tiamat, saving your lives,

'Call the Assembly, give me precedence over all the rest; and when you sit down to pass your decrees, cheerfully sit in Ubshukinna, the Hall of the Synod; now and for ever let my word be law;

'I, not you, will decide the world's nature, the things to come. My decrees shall never be altered, never annulled, but my creation endures to the ends of the world.'

III

Words broke from the lips of Anshar; he said to his counsellor Kaka,

'You are the counsellor in whom my heart finds its happiness, the one who judges truly and persuades fairly: go to Lahmu and Lahamu, I am sending you down to primeval sediments, call together the generations of the gods.

'Let them speak, let them sit down to banquet together, they shall eat the feast and drink the new-drawn liquor and then they shall all confirm in his destiny the avenger, Marduk! Kaka, go off, stand in front of them and repeat what I say.

'"I am sent here by your son Anshar, I am charged to tell you his secret thoughts,

"'She loathes us, our mother Tiamat has raised up that Company, she rages in turbulence and all have joined her, all those gods whom you begot,

"'Together they jostle the ranks to march with Tiamat, day and night furiously they plot, the growling roaring rout, ready for battle, while the Old Hag, the first mother, mothers a new brood.

"'She has loosed the irresistible missile, spawned enormous serpents with cutting fangs, chock-full of venom instead of blood, snarling dragons wearing their glory like gods. (Whoever sees this thing receives the shock of death, for when they heave those bodies up they never turn them back.)

> "'She has made the Worm
> the Dragon
> the Female Monster
> the Great Lion
> the Mad Dog
> the Man Scorpion
> the Howling Storm
> Kulili
> Kusariqu

"'There is no pity in their weapons, they do not flinch from battle for her law is binding, irrevocable.

"'Eleven monsters she has made, but she took from among the gods the clumsy labourer

KINGU

one of the first generation to be her Captain, War-leader, Assembly-leader, ordering the supplies, leading the van to battle

SUPREME COMMANDER OF THE WARS

All this she gave him when she set up their Company, she has said,

"'Now it is in your hands, my spell will hold them bound, they must obey my will. You are supreme, my one husband, *your* word will hold the rebel horde.'

"'She has given to him the Tables of Fate and fastened them on to his breast,

"'Now and for evermore your word is irrevocable, your judgements will last! They will quench the fire and the swinging mace will fail of its power.'

"'So Kingu has received the authority that belonged before to Anu, they have confirmed in their several natures the brood of monsters.

"'I sent Anu but he could not face her, Nudimmud came flying back in terror, then Marduk stood up, a wise god, one of your lineage, his heart has compelled him to set out and face Tiamat, but first he said this,

"'Creator of the gods who decides their destiny, if I must be your avenger, defeating Tiamat, saving your lives,

"'Call the Assembly, give me precedence over all the rest; and when you sit down to pass your decrees, cheerfully sit in Ubshukinna, the Hall of the Synod, now and for ever let my word be law;

"'I, not you, will decide the world's nature, the things to come. My decrees shall never be altered, never annulled, but my creation endures to the ends of the world.

"'Come soon and confirm the destiny of Marduk and the sooner he is off to meet the Great Adversary.'"'

He left and took his way down to Lahmu and Lahamu, stooping he kissed the primeval sediments, bowed to the ground at their feet and delivered the message to old gods,

'I have been sent here by your son Anu, I am charged to tell you his secret thoughts.

'She loathes us, our mother Tiamat has raised up that Company, she rages in turbulence and all have joined her, all those gods whom you begot.

'Together they jostle the ranks to march with Tiamat, day and night furiously they plot, the growling roaring rout, ready for battle, while the Old Hag, the first mother, mothers a new brood.

'She has loosed the irresistible missile, spawned enormous serpents with cutting fangs, chock-full of venom instead of blood, snarling dragons wearing their glory like gods. (Whoever sees this thing receives the shock of death, for when they heave those bodies up they never turn them back.)

> 'She has made the Worm
> the Dragon
> the Female Monster
> the Great Lion
> the Mad Dog
> the Man Scorpion
> the Howling Storm
> Kulili
> Kusariqu

'There is no pity in their weapons, they do not flinch from battle for her law is binding, irrevocable. Eleven such monsters she has made, but she took from among the gods the clumsy labourer

KINGU

one of the first generation to be her Captain, War-leader, Assembly-leader, ordering the supplies, leading the van to battle.

SUPREME COMMANDER OF THE WARS

All this she gave him when she raised their Company, she has said,

'"Now it is in your hands, my spell will hold them bound, they must obey my will. You are supreme my one husband, *your* word will hold the rebel horde."

'She has given to him the Tables of Fate and fastened them on to his breast,

'"Now and for evermore your word is irrevocable, your judgements will last! They will quench the fire and the swinging mace will fail of its power."

'So Kingu has received the authority that belonged before to Anu, they have confirmed in their several natures the brood of monsters.

'I sent Anu but he could not face her, Nudimmud came flying back in terror, then Marduk stood up, a wise god, one of your lineage, his heart has compelled him to set out and face Tiamat, but first he said this,

'"Creator of the gods who decides their destiny, if I must be your avenger, defeating Tiamat, saving your lives,

'"Call the Assembly, give me precedence over all the rest; and when you sit down to pass your decrees, cheerfully sit in Ubshukinna, the Hall of the Synod, now and for ever let my word be law;

'"I, not you, will decide the world's nature, the things to

come. My decrees shall never be altered, never annulled, but my creation endures to the ends of the world.

"'Come soon and confirm the destiny of Marduk and the sooner he is off to meet the Great Adversary.'"

When Lahmu and Lahamu heard this they muttered together, all the gods moaned with distress,
    'What a strange and terrible decision, the coil of Tiamat is too deep for us to fathom.'

Then they prepared for the journey, all the gods who determine the nature of the world and of things to come came in to Anshar, they filled Ubshukinna, greeted each other with a kiss.

In the Hall of the Synod the ancestral voices were heard, they sat down to the banquet, they ate the feast, they drank the new-drawn liquor and the tubes through which they sucked dripped with intoxicating wine.

Their souls expanded, their bodies grew heavy and drowsy; and this was the state of the gods when they settled the fate of Marduk.

IV

They set up a throne for Marduk and he sat down facing his forefathers to receive the government.

    'One god is greater than all great gods,
    a fairer fame, the word of command,
    the word from heaven, O Marduk,
    greater than all great gods, the honour
    and the fame, the will of Anu, great
    command, unaltering and eternal word!

Where there is action the first to act,
where there is government the first to govern;
to glorify some, to humiliate some,
that is the gift of the god.
Truth absolute, unbounded will;
which god dares question it?
In their beautiful places a place
is kept for you, Marduk, our avenger.

'We have called you here to receive the sceptre, to make you king of the whole universe. When you sit down in the Synod you are the arbiter; in the battle your weapon crushes the enemy.

'Lord, save the life of any god who turns to you; but as for the one who grasped evil, from that one let his life drain out.'

They conjured then a kind of apparition and made it appear in front of him, and they said to Marduk, the first-born son,

'Lord, your word among the gods arbitrates, destroys, creates: then speak and this apparition will disappear. Speak again, again it will appear.'

He spoke and the apparition disappeared. Again he spoke and it appeared again. When the gods had proved his word they blessed him and cried,

'MARDUK IS KING!'

They robed him in robes of a king, the sceptre and the throne they gave him, and matchless war-weapons as a shield against the adversary,

'Be off. Slit life from Tiamat, and may the winds carry her blood to the world's secret ends.'

The old gods had assigned to Bēl what he would be and what he should do, always conquering, always succeeding;

Then Marduk made a bow and strung it to be his own weapon, he set the arrow against the bow-string, in his right hand he grasped the mace and lifted it up, bow and quiver hung at his side, lightnings played in front of him, he was altogether an incandescence.

He netted a net, a snare for Tiamat; the winds from their quarters held it, south wind, north, east wind, west, and no part of Tiamat could escape.

With the net, the gift of Anu, held close to his side, he himself raised up

IMHULLU

the atrocious wind, the tempest, the whirlwind, the hurricane, the wind of four and the wind of seven, the tumid wind worst of all.

All seven winds were created and released to savage the guts of Tiamat, they towered behind him. Then the tornado

ABUBA

his last great ally, the signal for assault, he lifted up.

He mounted the storm, his terrible chariot, reins hitched to the side, yoked four in hand the appalling team, sharp poisoned teeth, the Killer, the Pitiless, Trampler, Haste, they knew arts of plunder, skills of murder.

He posted on his right the Batterer, best in the mêlée; on his left the Battle-fury that blasts the bravest, lapped in this armour, a leaping terror, a ghastly aureole; with a magic word clenched between his lips, a healing plant pressed in his palm, this lord struck out.

He took his route towards the rising sound of Tiamat's rage, and all the gods besides, the fathers of the gods pressed in around him, and the lord approached Tiamat.

He surveyed her scanning the Deep, he sounded the plan of Kingu her consort; but so soon as Kingu sees him he falters, flusters, and the friendly gods who filled the ranks beside him – when they saw the brave hero, their eyes suddenly blurred,

But Tiamat without turning her neck roared, spitting defiance from bitter lips,
    'Upstart, do you think yourself too great? Are they scurrying now from their holes to yours?'

Then the lord raised the hurricane, the great weapon, he flung his words at the termagant fury,
    'Why are you rising, your pride vaulting, your heart set on faction, so that sons reject fathers? Mother of all, why did you have to mother war?

    'You made that bungler your husband, Kingu! You gave him the rank, not his by right, of Anu. You have abused the gods my ancestors, in bitter malevolence you threaten Anshar, the king of all the gods.
    'You have marshalled forces for battle, prepared the war-tackle. Stand up alone and we will fight it out, you and I alone in battle.'

When Tiamat heard him her wits scattered, she was possessed and shrieked aloud, her legs shook from the crotch down, she gabbled spells, muttered maledictions, while the gods of war sharpened their weapons.

Then they met: Marduk, that cleverest of gods, and Tiamat grappled alone in single fight.

The lord shot his net to entangle Tiamat, and the pursuing

tumid wind, Imhullu, càme from behind and beat in her face.
When the mouth gaped open to suck him down he drove
Imhullu in, so that the mouth would not shut but wind raged
through her belly; her carcass blown up, tumescent, she gaped
– And now he shot the arrow that split the belly, that pierced
the gut and cut the womb.

Now that the Lord had conquered Tiamat he ended her life,
he flung her down and straddled the carcass; the leader was
killed, Tiamat was dead, her rout was shattered, her band
dispersed.

Those gods who had marched beside her now quaked in
terror, and to save their own lives, if they could, they turned
their backs on danger. But they were surrounded, held in a
tight circle, and there was no way out.

He smashed their weapons and tossed them into the net; they
found themselves inside the snare, they wept in holes and hid
in corners suffering the wrath of god.

When they resisted he put in chains the eleven monsters,
Tiamat's unholy brood, and all their murderous armament.
The demoniac band that marched in front of her he trampled
into the ground;

But Kingu the usurper, the chief of them, he bound and made
death's god. He took the Tables of Fate, usurped without
right, and sealed them with his seal to wear on his own breast.

When it was accomplished, the adversary vanquished, the
haughty enemy humiliated; when the triumph of Anshar was
accomplished on the enemy, and the will of Nudimmud was
fulfilled, then brave Marduk tightened the ropes of the
prisoners.

He turned back to where Tiamat lay bound, he straddled the

legs and smashed her skull (for the mace was merciless), he severed the arteries and the blood streamed down the north wind to the unknown ends of the world.

When the gods saw all this they laughed out loud, and they sent him presents. They sent him their thankful tributes.

The lord rested; he gazed at the huge body, pondering how to use it, what to create from the dead carcass. He split it apart like a cockle-shell; with the upper half he constructed the arc of sky, he pulled down the bar and set a watch on the waters, so they should never escape.

He crossed the sky to survey the infinite distance; he stationed himself above apsu, that apsu built by Nudimmud over the old abyss which now he surveyed, measuring out and marking in.

He stretched the immensity of the firmament, he made Esharra, the Great Palace, to be its earthly image, and Anu and Enlil and Ea had each their right stations.

V

He projected positions for the Great Gods conspicuous in the sky, he gave them a starry aspect as constellations; he measured the year, gave it a beginning and an end, and to each month of the twelve three rising stars.

When he had marked the limits of the year, he gave them Nebiru, the pole of the universe, to hold their course, that never erring they should not stray through the sky. For the seasons of Ea and Enlil he drew the parallel.

Through her ribs he opened gates in the east and west, and gave them strong bolts on the right and left; and high in the belly of Tiamat he set the zenith.

He gave the moon the lustre of a jewel, he gave him all the night, to mark off days, to watch by night each month the circle of a waxing waning light.

'New Moon, when you rise on the world, six days your horns are crescent, until half-circle on the seventh, waxing still phase follows phase, you will divide the month from full to full.

'Then wane, a gibbous light that fails, until low down on the horizon sun oversails you, drawing close his shadow lies across you, then dark of the moon – at thirty days the cycle's second starts again and follows through for ever and for ever.

'This is your emblem and the road you take, and when you close the sun, speak both of you with justice judgement uncorrupt . . .

[*some lines are missing here*]

When Marduk had sent out the moon, he took the sun and set him to complete the cycle from this one to the next New Year. . . . He gave him the Eastern Gate, and the ends of the night with the day, he gave to Shamash.

Then Marduk considered Tiamat. He skimmed spume from the bitter sea, heaped up the clouds, spindrift of wet and wind and cooling rain, the spittle of Tiamat.

With his own hands from the steaming mist he spread the clouds. He pressed hard down the head of water, heaping mountains over it, opening springs to flow: Euphrates and Tigris rose from her eyes, but he closed the nostrils and held back their springhead.

He piled huge mountains on her paps and through them drove water-holes to channel the deep sources; and high overhead he arched her tail, locked-in to the wheel of heaven; the pit was under his feet, between was the crotch, the sky's fulcrum. Now the earth had foundations and the sky its mantle.

When god's work was done, when he had fashioned it all and finished, then on earth he founded temples and made them over to Ea;

But the Tables of Destiny taken from Kingu he returned as a first greeting to Anu; and those gods who had hung up their weapons defeated, whom he had scattered, now fettered, he drove into his presence, the father of the gods.

With the weapons of war broken, he bound to his foot the eleven, Tiamat's monstrous creation. He made likenesses of them all and now they stand at the gate of the abyss, the Apsu Gate; he said,
    'This is for recollection for Tiamat shall not be forgotten.'

All the generations of the Great Gods when they saw him were full of joy, with Lahmu and Lahamu; their hearts bounded when they came over to meet him.

King Anshar made him welcome with ceremony, Anu and Enlil came carrying presents; but when his mother Damkina sent her present, then he glowed, an incandescence lit his face.

He gave to her servant Usmu, who brought the greeting, charge of the secret house of Apsu; he made him warden of the sanctuaries of Eridu.

All the heavenly gods were there, all the Igigi fell prostrate in front of him, all that were there of the Anunnaki kissed his feet. The whole order came in together to worship.

They stood in front of him, low they bowed and they shouted

'He is king indeed!'

When all the gods in their generations were drunk with the glamour of the manhood of Marduk, when they had seen his clothing spoiled with the dust of battle, then they made their act of obedience . . .

He bathed and put on clean robes, for he was their king. . . . A glory was round his head; in his right hand he held the mace of war, in his left grasped the sceptre of peace, the bow was slung on his back; he held the net, and his glory touched the abyss . . .

He mounted the throne raised up in the temple. Damkina and Ea and all the Great Gods, all the Igigi shouted,

'In time past Marduk meant only "the beloved son" but now he is king indeed, this is so!'

They shouted together,

'GREAT LORD OF THE UNIVERSE!

this is his name, in him we trust.'

When it was done, when they had made Marduk their king, they pronounced peace and happiness for him,

'Over our houses you keep unceasing watch, and all you wish from us, that will be done.'

Marduk considered and began to speak to the gods assembled in his presence. This is what he said,

'In the former time you inhabited the void above the abyss, but I have made Earth as the mirror of Heaven, I have consolidated the soil for the foundations, and there I will build my city, my beloved home.

'A holy precinct shall be established with sacred halls for the presence of the king. When you come up from the deep to join the Synod you will find lodging and sleep by night.

'When others from heaven descend to the Assembly, you too will find lodging and sleep by night. It shall be

BABYLON

the home of the gods. The masters of all the crafts shall build it according to my plan.'

When the older of the gods had heard this speech they had still one question to ask:

'Over these things that your hands have formed, who will administer law? Over all this earth that you have made, who is to sit in judgement?

'You have given your Babylon a lucky name, let it be our home for ever! Let the fallen gods day after day serve us; and as we enforce your will let no one else usurp our office.'

Marduk, Tiamat's conqueror, was glad; the bargain was good; he went on speaking his arrogant words explaining it all to the gods,

'They will perform this service, day after day, and you shall enforce my will as law.'

Then the gods worshipped in front of him, and to him again, to the king of the whole universe they cried aloud,

'This great lord was once our son, now he is our king. We invoked him once for very life, he who is the lord, the blaze of light, the sceptre of peace and of war the mace.

'Let Ea be his architect and draw the excellent plan, his bricklayers are we!'

VI

Now that Marduk has heard what it is the gods are saying, he
is moved with desire to create a work of consummate art. He
told Ea the deep thought in his heart.

> 'Blood to blood
> I join,
> blood to bone
> I form
> an original thing,
> its name is MAN,
> aboriginal man
> is mine in making.

> 'All his occupations
> are faithful service,
> the gods that fell
> have rest,
> I will subtly alter
> their operations,
> divided companies
> equally blest.'

Ea answered with carefully chosen words, completing the plan
for the gods' comfort. He said to Marduk,
    'Let one of the kindred be taken; only one need die for
the new creation. Bring the gods together in the Great Assem-
bly; there let the guilty die, so the rest may live.'

Marduk called the Great Gods to the Synod; he presided
courteously, he gave instructions and all of them listened with
grave attention.

The king speaks to the rebel gods,

'Declare on your oath if ever before you spoke the truth, who instigated rebellion? Who stirred up Tiamat? Who led the battle? Let the instigator of war be handed over; guilt and retribution are on him, and peace will be yours for ever.'

The Great Gods answered the Lord of the Universe, the king and counsellor of gods,

'It was Kingu who instigated rebellion, he stirred up that sea of bitterness and led the battle for her.'

They declared him guilty, they bound and held him down in front of Ea, they cut his arteries and from his blood they created man; and Ea imposed his servitude.

When it was done, when Ea in his wisdom had created man and man's burden, this thing was past comprehension, this marvel of subtlety conceived by Marduk and executed by Nudimmud.

Then Marduk, as king, divided the gods: one host below and another above, three hundred above for the watchers of heaven, watchers of the law of Anu; five times sixty for earth, six hundred gods between earth and heaven.

When universal law was set up and the gods allotted their calling, then the Anunnaki, the erstwhile fallen, opened their mouths to speak to Marduk:

'Now that you have freed us and remitted our labour how shall we make a return for this? Let us build a temple and call it

THE-INN-OF-REST-BY-NIGHT

'There we will sleep at the season of the year, at the Great Festival when we form the Assembly; we will build altars for him, we will build the Parakku, the Sanctuary.'

When Marduk heard this his face shone like broad day:

'Tall Babel Tower, it shall be built as you desire; bricks shlla be set in moulds and you shall name it Parakku, the Sanctuary.'

The Anunnaki gods took up the tools, one whole year long they set bricks in moulds; by the second year they had raised its head ESAGILA, it towered, the earthly temple, the symbol of infinite heaven.

Inside were lodgings for Marduk and Enlil and Ea. Majestically he took his seat in the presence of them all, where the head of the ziggurat looked down to the foot.

When that building was finished the Anunnaki built themselves chapels; then all came in together and Marduk set out the banquet.

> 'This is Babylon,
> "dear city of god"
> your beloved home!
> The length and breadth
> are yours, possess it,
> enjoy it, it is your own.'

When all the gods sat down together there was wine and feasting and laughter; and after the banquet in beautiful Esagila they performed the liturgy from which the universe receives its structure, the occult is made plain, and through the universe gods are assigned their places.

When the Fifty Great Gods had sat down with the Seven who design the immutable nature of things, they raised up three hundred into heaven. It was then too that Enlil lifted the bow of Marduk and laid it in front of them.

He also lifted the net; they praised the workmanship now that they saw the intricacy of the net and the beauty of the bow.

Anu lifted the bow and kissed it, he said before all the gods,
   'This is my daughter.'
And this was the naming of the bow –

> 'One is for Long-wood,
> two for the Rain-bow,
> three is for Starry-bow
> glittering above.'

And Starry-bow was a god among gods.

When Anu had pronounced the bow's triple destiny he lifted up the king's throne and set Marduk above in the gods' Assembly.

Among themselves they uttered an execration, by oil and by water, pricking their throats, to abide its fate on pain of death.

They ratified his authority as King of Kings, Lord of the Lords of the Universe. Anshar praised him, he called him ASARLUHI, the name that is first, the highest name.

> 'We will wait and listen, we bend and worship
> his name! His word is the last appeal
> his writ will run from the zenith to the pit.
> All glory to the son, our avenger!
> His empire has no end, shepherd of men,
> he made them his creatures to the last of time,
> they must remember.
> He shall command hecatombs, for the gods,
> they shall commend food, for the fathers,
> and cherish the sanctuary
> where the odour of incense and whisper of liturgy
> echo on earth the customs of heaven.
> Black-headed men will adore him on earth,
> the subjected shall remember their god,
> at his word they shall worship the goddess.

Let offerings of food not fail
for god and goddess, at his command.
Let them serve the gods, at his command,
work their lands, build their houses.
Let black-headed men serve the gods on earth
without remission; while as for us,
in the multitude of his names
he is our god.
Let us hail him in his names,
let us hail him by his fifty names,
one god.'

The Hymn of the Fifty Names of Marduk

MARDUK is One,
he is Son of the Sun,
he is the first, the sunburst.

Pasture and pool,
and the byres full,
torrents of rain that hammered the enemy.

Most shining one,
Son of the Sun,
the gods are walking always in the flame of his light.

He created man
a living thing
to labour for ever, and gods go free,

to make to break
to love and to save,
to Marduk all power and praise!

MARUKKA is Two
hammering out the whole creation
to ease the gods in tribulation.

MARUTUKKU is Three,
his praises are heard on every hand,
the armed child who shields the land.

BARASHAKUSHU is Fourth,
who stood at need to bridle earth,
his spirit stoops, his heart is love.

LUGALDIMMERANKIA is Five,
King of the Cosmos!
Over the universe he is acclaimed
by that Great Company his wrath had shamed
Almighty God!

NARI is Six, the Deliverer,
he is our conscience, for once
in our trouble he brought us peace
and a safe haven;
Anunnaki, Igigi, from the pit
and in heaven,
hearing this name secretly quake.

ASARULUDU is Seven,
the Great Magician, this title came from Anu;
in time of peril, their good leader,
by the deadly duel he fetched them rest.

NAMTILLAKU is Eight,
in the shadow of death he discovered life;
it was as though they were made
all new; conjured from death at his word until
the reckless rout submit to his will.

NAMRU is Nine, the gods go a-walking
in the furnace of his beauty.

Voices of older days have spoken: Lahmu, Lahamu, Anshar

have spoken, each of them uttered three names; they said to the children,

    'Three names he has from each of us, three names he needs from you.'

As once before in Synod in Ubshukinna, at the place of decision, the young gods eagerly talked together,

    'He is the hero, our son, our avenger, we will praise the name of our defender.'

They sat down together to shape his destiny, and all of them chanted his names in the Sanctuary.

VII

The Hymn, continued

ASARU cultivates the sown,
conducts water by small channels
for seed-time, for shooting green
and harvest grain.

ASARUALIM, the gods in fear and hope
at Council turn to him.
He is the light, ASARUALIM NUNNA,
light of the glory of his father;
he is the law of Anu and Enlil and Ea,
he is fullness and plenty,
the gods grow fat on his bounty.

TUTU is life renewed
that sweetens the sanctuary; should wrath
once more rouse up their company
he teaches them to repeat the charm

that lulls to sleep,
he has no peer in that Assembly.

ZIUKKINNA lives in every god,
he made the skies their happiness,
he holds them to their bliss;
below the clouds dull men
remember him,

for this is ZIKU the kernel of life,
sweet breath of grace, abundance,
benevolence, unbelievable wealth
changing famine to plenty;
we breathed his sweetness
in our extremity.
We will speak of the mighty,
we will sing the song of his glory.

AGAKU, the love and the wrath,
with living words he quickens the dead,
he pitied fallen gods,
remitted the labour laid on the adversary.
For your relief he made mankind, his words
endure, he is kind, he has power
of life, it is in the mouth
of black-headed men who remember him.

But also this is TUKU,
they mutter his anathemas
who overwhelmed evil
with mysterious words.

As SHAZU he made the heart,
he sees the marrow,
no sinner escapes his scrutiny.

He has formed the Assembly and spread
   his protection,
he oversees justice and subdues rebellion,
he has rooted out malice;
wherever he goes the wrong and the right
stand separate.

As one who reads the heart this too
is ZISI, a name that hushed the rebel horde,
out of the body of older gods
drove freezing fear, freeing his fathers, for

SUHRIM is the missile
that extinguished them,
the abject band that cringe from him,
their schemes forestalled, and flying
in the wind.
Be glad you gods, be glad!

He is SUHGURIM who can destroy,
but is an open court to hear all causes;
old gods created new, the enemy erased
and to the children's children
nothing is left of them
or what they did; his name alone
answers the summons of the world.

ZAHRIM, the destroyer, lives!
Iniquity is dead, he has found out
the enemy; when the gods fled
he brought them home, each
to his own, and by this name is known.

ZAHGURIM, saviour destroyer,
terrible title, his enemy is fallen
as it were on the field of battle.

ENBILULU, health to the gods and wealth!
He called their names, he called
for hecatombs roast in flames,
he planned the pastures,
sank wells and freed the waters.

He is EPADUN gathering moisture
from sky and earth to wash down the furrows,
watering ploughland with sluices
with dams and dykes in irrigation.

Enbilulu is hymned as GUGAL,
in the orchards of the gods
he watches the canals, he fills
the store-room with sesame, emmer,
abundant grain.

And he is HEGAL,
heaping up wealth for all people,
into the world he sends sweet rain
and greenness . . .

As SIRSIR he seized the carcass,
he carried off Chaos meshed in his snare,
and heaped on her mountains.
Overseer of the world and faithful shepherd,
where his brow is furrowed,
like a shock of hair the corn
waves up; where the vast ocean
rises in anger, he vaults her as a bridge
thrown over the place where duel was
    fought.

He is also called MALAH, and many another;
the sour sea is his skiff who captains the hulk.

A heap of grain is GIL, barley and sesame
doled out for the land's good.

This is GILMA, the unquenchable fire
that tempers the eternity of their dwelling,
and for their safety is braced as the hoop
    holding the barrel.

This is AGILMA,
who from the tearing surf creates
over the waters clouds
to guard the unchanging sky.

ZULUM cuts into clay,
allots the acres, grants the tithes.

This MUMMU is the creative word,
the life of the universe.

GISHNUMUNAB, the seed, created
races of men from the world's quarters.
From the wreck of Tiamat's rout,
from the stuff of fallen gods
he made mankind.

He is LUGALABDUBUR
who came as king to confront Chaos,
her forces wither before him for he is steadfast,
the foundations are firm in every direction.

PAPALGUENNA, Lord of Lords,
most sublime god, he rules his brothers.

LUGALDURMAH, at the navel of the world
where heaven and earth are held
by the cord; where the high gods gather,
his greatness ranks higher than all.

ARANUNNA, Counsellor, with his father Ea
peerless in his sovereign manner,
he created gods.

DUMUDUKU is the bright mountain,
Dumuduku, the presence in the temple,
at the place of decision where nothing is
    decided
except with him.

LUGALLANNA, he is strong
with the charge of heaven,
conspicuous among gods
even more than Anshar who called him out,
called one from all.

LUGALUGGA, King Death!
He took them at the crisis, in the maelstrom;
the encompassing intellect, the mind full-
    stretched.

IRKINGU, in the battle-fury he bore away the
    bungler;
he created law and law now rules creation.

KINMA, adviser and leader,
his name strikes terror in gods,
the roar of the tornado.

ESIZKUR, up there he sits
in the chapel of prayer, at the Great Festival,
when the gods all come, presents are given, duties
    imposed.
Unless he is by nothing is created
subtle or beautiful, but when he would
man was made in the quarters of the world,

without him the gods
would not know their hour.

He is GIBIL, the furnace in which the point
is tempered; lightnings forged
the weapons of war against Tiamat;
the gods will never sound
the reaches of his mind.

His name is also ADDU,
wet weather and the welcome storm,
the kindly roar of thunder
hovering over earth.
After the storm the clouds break up
at his word, and under heaven
all people daily have their bread from him.

ASHARU guides the gods of Fate;
all other gods he guards.

As NEBIRU he projected the stars
in their orbit, the wandering gods obey
the laws of passage.
Nebiru, at the still centre,
is the god they adore;
of this starry one they say

> 'He who once crossed the firmament
>   tirelessly
> now is the nub of the universe,
> and all the other gods hold course
> on him; he shall fold
> the gods like a flock
> and conquer Tiamat.
> Let her life be narrow and short,

> let her recede into the future
> far-off from man-kind,
> till time is old, keep her
> for ever absent.'

Because he had moulded matter and created the ether, Enlil
his father, named him
Bēl Mātāti, Lord of this World.
With his own name he signed him when the gods of heaven had
ended the hymn.

Now too Ea having heard rejoiced,
    'The Great Gods have glorified my son, he is Ea, named
by my name, he will execute my will and direct my rites.'

HANSHA!

With fifty names the gods proclaimed him.

HANSHA!

With fifty they named him, the one who is first and fares
farthest!

Epilogue

Remember the Titles of Marduk!

Rulers will recite them, wise men and sages debate them, father
to son repeat them, even shepherds and herdsmen shall hear
them.

Let men rejoice in Marduk! The prince of the gods. Man and
earth will prosper, for his rule is strong, his command is firm,
none of the gods can alter his will; where his eyes have fixed
they do not falter.

There is no god can bear his anger, his intellect is vast and his benevolence; sinners and such trash he will blast in his presence; not so the wise teacher to whose words we listen; he wrote it down, he saved it for time to come.

Let the Igigi who built his dwelling, let the gods speak: this was the song of Marduk who defeated Tiamat and attained sovereignty.

Note on *The Sumerian Underworld*

THIS poem was found on a damaged and weathered tablet, and the end is quite illegible. A German translation was published by E. Ebeling in *Orientalia*, 18 (1949), p. 285, entitled 'A Description of the Underworld in the Sumerian Language'; it is a song of self-praise by some unnamed god of the underworld.

THE SUMERIAN UNDERWORLD

There stands a house under the mountain of the world,
a road runs down, the mountain covers it
and no man knows the way. It is a house
that binds bad men with ropes
and clamps them into a narrow space.
It is a house that separates the wicked
and the good; this is a house from out of which
no one escapes, but just men need not fear before its judge,
for in this river of spent souls the good
shall never die although the wicked perish.
This is my house, on its foundations stand
the mountains of the sunrise, but who shall see
into the pit? It is a house that separates
the wicked and the just; it is a house
that smothers in clay the souls that come to it.
It is the house of the setting sun,
the pallid god in livid splendour; the sill
is a monster with jaws that gape
and the jambs of the doors are a sharp knife
to slash down wicked men. The two rims
of the river of hell are the rapier thrust
of terror, a raging lion guards it
and who can face his fury? Here also lie
the rainbow gardens of the Lady.

Introduction to Inanna's Journey to Hell

The Sumerian liturgies, as scholars have translated them and interpreted them for us, remain so obscure and remote that one can hardly enter them imaginatively, as one dares to enter even poetry as remote·as the Iliad. *Yet, in exploring the far vistas opened by lines of such magic as those of Milton . . . concerning Proserpine . . . one is quickened to participate in the impassioned experience of a collective emotion, vast, cumulative and ancient.*

Maud Bodkin, *Archetypal Patterns in Poetry*

These words, written in 1934, challenge the translator. How far is it still true that Sumerian writings are so obscure and remote that we can 'hardly enter them imaginatively'? The last thirty-six years have added a very large store to what was before a meagre collection of hymns, and fragments of narrative, myth and liturgy. Parts of a much later semitic version of *Inanna's Journey to Hell* were already known, but nothing of the Sumerian prototype, which was not published until 1937, and then only a part of the whole myth as we know it now. In all some 5,000 Sumerian tablets and fragments exist today, and only about a third of them have been published. Nearly all date from around the eighteenth century B.C., though they were probably composed some time before that, since Sumerian literature goes back to the mid third millennium. Parts of at least twenty Sumerian myths are known. They recount the creation and organization of the universe, the birth of the gods, the creation of man, the flood, and the enigma and mystery of death.

In the long poem of *Inanna's Journey* many of the great

archetypal themes are joined: the descent to hell, the sevenfold approach, death and rebirth, the pursuit, the mourning women. This conjunction is in itself surprising, and it is very much more surprising on such an early morning of our human history. Our poem can be divided into the tale of Inanna's descent to hell, and her confrontation with the Queen of Hell, Ereshkigal; her 'death' followed by rescue and return to earth accompanied by a horde of devils; the substitute she finds to take her place in hell, the condemnation of her husband Dumūzi to his fate, his flight and pursuit by the devils, his death and the mourning by his mother, wife and sister.

The goddess Inanna (the name is sometimes rendered Innin) is not at all the warlike, starry semitic Ishtar who succeeded her, but a more homely goddess of the fertile earth. Her name links her with the granary and byre; she is also sometimes the Lady of the Date Clusters, and Lady of Heaven. It is a very characteristic ambiguity. Inanna is the sister of the sun-god Utu, who is also a more domestic and earthy character than his semitic counterpart Shamash, though both were looked on as judges of men. Most crucially for the plot of this poem, she is the younger sister of Ereshkigal, whose name means 'Lady of the Great Earth', or 'Queen of Hell'. A fragment of Sumerian cosmogony was quoted on p. 33, which tells of the beginning

When Anu took for himself the heavens,
When Enlil took for himself the earth,
When Ereshkigal had taken the Underworld for her portion ...

Dumuzi's name means 'true son'; he is called the Shepherd, but in many marriage songs he is addressed as *Ama-ushamgal-anna*, which seems to mean 'the power that is in the date palm'. In the laments he is sometimes *Damu*, 'the Child'. It is as a shepherd caring for flocks and folds, bringing in milk and cream, in love with the song of flutes, that he appears in the

poem of Inanna's journey. But some of the hymns also invoke
him as the life-giving waters that return in early spring, and
the rising sap. It is the same ambiguity as with Inanna; their
characters blur at the edges, unlike the Tammuz of later
semitic religions, who was far more limited in power and
function.

There are a number of courting and marriage songs in
honour of Inanna, some of the former are contests or flytings
between her suitors, the farmer and the shepherd (Dumuzi);
these are far-off forerunners of the contesting shepherds of
Theocritos, of Daphnis and Polyphemos; they may also very
well be a comic matrix out of which has come the tragic contest
of Cain and Abel. The marriage songs are richly sensuous, the
imagery drawn from the flocks, the fields, gardens and orchards,
and the teeming rivers. Some can be matched, phrase for phrase,
with the Song of Songs or Canticles; and Professor Kramer sees
in the latter, traditional songs accompanying a sacred marriage
borrowed by the Hebrews from their Canaanite neighbours,
and so looking back to Assyria and Babylon. On the other
hand they could as well be spontaneous and natural responses
to a similar situation:

> These are for you,
> the temple of the earth,
> a beacon in Eridu,
> brilliance of the moon's bright place
> the gateway to my house,
> my house where love has entered.
> It has a lucky name, it floats
> a drifting cloud. In the house
> there is a mighty shrine,
> pure from the furnace,
> in the shrine there is a bed,
> inlaid with the blue-black lapis,
> they are for you ...

> Now the sun sleeps, day is done,
> this was your day,
> it is time for bed and the bridegroom comes ...

So goes the beginning of one of these songs; the translation is freely based on S. N. Kramer and Thorkild Jacobsen.[1] Inanna was the Lady of Uruk, the 'Erech' of the Bible, its own especial goddess. Probably some time in the third millennium, when the Sumerian city-states were becoming self-conscious, with kings instead of councils to govern them, the king of Uruk came to be thought of as the husband of the goddess. Their marriage ensured the fecundity and prosperity of the land. Later an actual marriage was almost certainly consummated (not only in Uruk) between the king of the city and the goddess, in the person of her priestess. When this happened at Ur, and perhaps Badtibira, the king was addressed as Dumuzi. In July, three months after Dumuzi's marriage, his death was marked with rites of weeping and lamentations. The chief mourners were three women: Dumuzi's wife Inanna, his mother Ninsun and his sister Geshtinanna. Ninsun may once have meant the deified ewe; she has some of the most beautiful laments in which he is called on as Damu, 'the Child', her child. Geshtinanna is the Lady of the Vine, or the Vine of Heaven. In *Inanna's Journey* she is also the wise singer 'who understands the song', wise too in letters and in interpreting dreams. If the last lines of the poem are understood correctly she also descended to hell, and there she may have remained in place of her brother. If this were so it would explain her semitic name *Bēlit-Sēri* which means, like the Sumerian *Nin-Edin*, Lady of the Wilderness, Lady of Desolation – another name for the place of death, the Underworld. It explains too how she

1. *Proceedings of the American Philosophical Society*, 107 (1963), p. 501; and *Religions in Antiquity*, ed. J. Neusner, Dartmouth College, 1966, p. 24.

comes to be the Book-keeper of Heaven and Earth and the Recorder of Hell.

II

So much of *Inanna's Journey* is concerned with death and the underworld that we ought to try and get a little nearer to what the Sumerians meant by these words, if it is at all possible. This underworld is not quite the same as the hell of the Akkadian poems; it is not like that seen by Enkidu in a vision, before his death in *The Epic of Gilgamesh*. One of the Sumerian names is *kur*, 'the Mountain', a foreign and an alien place; it was also 'the Great City', great because its inhabitants are all the people who have ever lived, the population of the past; and it was the Land-of-No-Return that carries the same admonishment, almost the same hopeless words as Dante's

> Lasciate ogni speranza voi ch'entrate ...

The topography is indistinct. There is one poem called *The Sumerian Underworld* (see p. 115) that sets out to describe it. Here is the recurrent image of hell's gate as the dragon with jaws gaping, but the door-jambs sharp as knives, and the horror of the river bank as slippery and sharp as the rapier blade, are its own. The guarding 'Cerberus' is a raging lion, but there are 'rainbow gardens of the Lady [Inanna]', like Virgil's asphodel meadow, for the refreshment of the dead. There was darkness in this hell, but it was not eternal darkness, for after setting on earth the sun travelled all night through the underworld until dawn; and because on earth he was the great judge of living men, he also judged the dead during his underworld sojourn, allotting punishment and rewards. These dead were not treated all alike; there were gradations and hierarchies, punishment for the wicked, while 'the virtuous soul need not fear before that judge'.

Inanna did not have to cross the 'man-devouring' river sometimes called Hubur. In *The Babylonian Creation* Hubur is a name for Tiamat, the cosmic waters of the abyss; it is the ditch of hell that sometimes stands simply for death, as in the prayer, 'He drew me forth from the river [Hubur]'.[2] In some of the laments for Dumuzi it is a great river that bears him away, and his mother stands on the bank straining after him, unable to follow, like the women weeping for Tammuz and Adonis on the banks of other rivers. To enter the dark lapis lazuli palace of Ereshkigal, Inanna had to pass through the seven gates of the seven walls of the city; walls and gates that other ages transferred to heaven. At the centre of these seven 'circles' Ereshkigal sat stark naked on her throne. She had had husbands – one was Nergal, the plague god; and the seven Anunnaki, gods of destiny in the upper world and so of doom in the nether world, were her companions; while order was kept by certain grim messengers, the *gallē* or constables. In another poem about Inanna, the Anunnaki are likened to bats,

> O my lady, the Anunna, the great gods,
> fluttering like bats fly off from before you to the clefts . . .[3]

It might be the spirits of the suitors killed by Odysseus when Hermes leads them to Hades, 'gibbering like bats that squeak and flutter in the depths of some mysterious cave . . .'[4]

The Sumerian underworld is not so very unlike Homer's

2. For this and other epithets and personal names, see K. Tallqvist, 'Sumerisch-Akkadische Namen der Totenwelt', *Studia Orientalia*, 5 (1934).

3. W. Hallo and J. Van Dijk, *The Exaltation of Inanna*, 1968, lines 34–5.

4. *Odyssey*, XXIV, 6–7, trans. Rieu.

House of Hades or Hesiod's Tartaros. A seventh-century Greek would not have been too much startled at finding himself in Ereshkigal's kingdom; many of the landmarks would have been what he expected. Rather different, and to a contemporary reader more penetrating, is the Waste Land imagery. In this land of the dead the idea of heat and fire is notably absent, but water and dust are there; Inanna's great fear is to be drowned under the dust of hell.

These horrifying images are most likely to have come from what men actually saw and knew of death and its circumstances. Pestilence and famine were frequent; death could come suddenly in the flooding of rivers, or lingeringly by drought. The fields and pastures of the two river lands are bordered by the unsown where sandstorms curdled and many men must have died slowly and agonizingly of thirst – their dry bones, scoured by the wind, lying as memorials for other travellers; so the desert, the *edin*, is simply a name for death and hell, the valley of bones. Another Sumerian word, *arali*, is of unknown etymology but its meaning is equally clear: it is the desolation of the Waste Land,

> Here is no water but only rock
> rock and no water and the sandy road . . .

The Sumerians would have surely recognized that place. There is a beautiful group of laments all of which begin with the same line: *Edin-naū-sag-gā*, 'In the desert . . .' or 'In the dead land . . .' It was in the *edin* that tragedy overtook Dumuzi, coming in a hot wind with dust storms that destroy the flocks and the fold:

> As whirlwinds from the south pass through, so it cometh from
>   the desert, from a terrible land,
> A grievous vision . . .

The imagery is the same and so is the foreboding in Isaiah's 'burden of the desert of the sea', written in the years of exile in Babylon.

In one lament which I have filched for this sequence, Dumuzi, who has been carried away to death's kingdom, answers his mother,

> Though the grass will shoot
>   from the land
> I am not grass, I cannot come
>   to her calling.
> The waters rise for her,
> I am not water to come
>   for her wailing,
> I am not shoots of grass
>   in a dead land.

This is not so far from the anonymous *Lament for Bion*, who himself wrote a Greek *Lament for Adonis* which imitates the laments for Tammuz, and so leads us straight back to Dumuzi, the young shepherd.

> Mallows, and tangled anise, and the grass-
> green parsley die, and in the garden vanish,
> but shoot again with the new year. Not so
> with us, strong men and obstinate and wise;
> once dead we lie in holes of earth and slide
> into a sleep from which no one will wake.

... All flesh is grass ... the grass withereth, the flower fadeth. .... The thought may be banal now, but once it was fresh. In the Sumerian mourning song we catch the tremor of that freshness.

III

Inanna's Journey is too simple and universal to need any special commentary. There are fewer problems than, for instance, in *The Babylonian Creation*, and the two latest additions to the text have almost solved the enigma of the goddess's decision to make the fatal journey in the first place; and the question of Dumuzi's 'return'. Apart from these there are a few odd or perplexing matters about which something might be said.

First we begin in the middle of the story, for Inanna is already Dumuzi's wife. The time is either July when, in later times, Tammuz was mourned, or it is August, the month of purification and of the goddess Ishtar's descent to the underworld. In either case it is the hot dry season of anxiety, the time of scarce water and parched food when there might easily arise thoughts of the dead returning to eat with the living, an All Souls' Feast. Inanna goes down to hell fully armed, as for a duel, with all her powers and prerogatives, the symbols and insignia of a great goddess. Because of the description of the sevenfold stripping of the goddess it has been thought that a dramatic action is described with at its centre the stripping of a surrogate, living or statue. At the gate of hell she commits a sin: instead of giving the true reason for her coming she tells a concocted story which takes in nobody. When naked and stripped of all her powers and adornments she falls on her knees before Ereshkigal and 'dies', only Enki takes pity on her; the other great gods apparently think that she has got what she deserves.

The grotesque and primitive mode of creation by Enki of the Kalaturrū and Kurgarrū who are to rescue her, is probably made necessary to circumvent some magical sanction imposed by Ereshkigal to prevent just such a rescue. These are not creatures of flesh and blood but, like the beautiful and fanciful beings of fairy-tale and folklore that can be made to vanish at a word into dust, they are appearances only and, to judge by the later semitic poem of 'Ishtar's Descent', they are sexless. This may in fact be the source of their power in the underworld. There were also orders of priesthood with these names whose members were eunuchs. It is tempting to see in the distress of Ereshkigal when she lies naked moaning, and which the Kurgarru and Kalaturru are sent to relieve, a direct result of confining in her sterile kingdom the goddess of all the generative forces of the earth, but the text is difficult at this point. The warning against eating or drinking in the underworld is the one ignored by Persephone, whose captivity to Hades was made absolute when she ate the pomegranate seed, but is observed by Piper Steenie in *Wandering Willie's Tale* when he is warned to take neither meat nor drink nor silver in the ghastly hell-vision of Redgauntlet Hall. This popular wisdom, practical nursery lore, could be counted on in the audience of the *Adapa* story in order that they should enjoy its *dénouement* (p. 169).

The devils who come up to the daylight clinging to Inanna enforce those most ancient laws that cannot be flouted even by gods, like the Erinyes, or the Constable of the Harlequinade. I suspect also that they should have some of the comic exaggeration and vulgar speech of medieval devils.

Up to the point where Dumuzi commits the sin of *hubris* and is condemned by Inanna, the poem exists in one main version, but for his pursuit and death there are at least two alternative but overlapping versions (see p. 132 below). The order of events becomes confused; but in all accounts Dumuzi, like another Orestes, flies from his pursuers, appeals to the sun as the just judge, is helped by his sister and finally dies. Because of this overlapping it is impossible to say how long the pursuit went on or how many times he appealed to Utu. Kramer has pointed out that since he carried his soul to the home of Geshtinanna it shows that the soul of one such as was Dumuzi, was thought of as indestructible, in spite of the fact that his body could be so changed. It was the soul not the body which continued to exist in the underworld, much like Homer's 'strengthlcss shades of the dead'.[5]

The poem of 'Dumuzi's Dream', has an alternative account of his pursuit and death.

When the long pursuit ended with the capture of Dumuzi and when he was carried away to the underworld by the devils, it was then that the lament began. The singers are the mother, the wife and the sister, but they are as interchangeable as their songs – which is hardly surprising, for the mother who mourns a son has mourned a husband and very likely a brother too. The songs are liturgical; they use stereotyped images, but whether or not they were acted out by the mourners, like the *Quem quaeritis?* of the medieval Easter liturgy, we do not know. The peculiar combinations of direct speech and of description of the action, as though by a narrator, come nearer to libretto than any other literary form.

Although the texts of *Inanna's Journey* and the pursuit of Dumuzi do not actually include any of the laments, the last lines of one of the Ur fragments, which has recently been added to the poem, describe Geshtinanna wandering through the city 'like a bird complaining' on account of her brother, which may have introduced, and which gives the occasion to add, one or two of these mourning songs. In the first a now contrite and desolate Inanna mourns her young husband. This comes from the laments called by Thorkild Jacobsen the 'Herder' series, because in them Dumuzi is mourned as a young bull. Then I have chosen the most beautiful and poignant of all the songs: *The Reed-flute Dirge* – 'My heart is piping in the wilderness...' to bring back to mind the terrible moment when Inanna, just risen from hell, turns over Dumuzi to the devils and 'the flute-

5. *Iraq*, 22 (1960), p. 68, note o.25.

song of the shepherd is broken'. Then comes a dialogue between the mother and her dead son and, quoting Professor Jacobsen, 'there is in all the Tammuz literature no picture of more complete and utter grief than the one in the reed-flute lament, of the mother who goes slowly and alone up to her son's body, shudders, looks at his face, and has only this to say: "You look different."'[6]

Inanna's is the first of the tragic journeys to hell of which we know, and it had seemed to be motiveless. She is not 'loth to go', torn from the Nysian plain, or,

> . . . from that fair field
> Of Enna, where Proserpine, gathering flow'rs,
> Herself a fairer flower, by gloomy Dis
> Was gathered, which cost Ceres all that pain
> To seek her through the world . . .

There is no rape; she is not Persephone. If Persephone is to be found at all in this company it is on the throne of Ereshkigal. The underworld journeys of mortal, or semi-divine, heroes were always undertaken for some concrete purpose: to fetch back some person or thing, to learn a truth or gain a reward. So it was with Theseus, Heracles, Odysseus, Orpheus, Psyche, Virgil, Dante; but Inanna, 'from the "Great Above" set her mind on the "Great Below"' as Kramer's translation of the first line has it, and that is all there is to it, or was until very recently. There is of course Enlil's sour reply to the appeal for help on Inanna's behalf – 'My daughter is insatiable, she has brought it on herself' – with its implication that she had wished to usurp her sister's throne; but a recent commentator has translated the line in which Ereshkigal mounts her throne as a preliminary to the judges pronouncing sentence of death on Inanna, in a sense in which a furious Inanna flings her sister

6. 'Toward the Image of Tammuz', *History of Religions*, I, 2, (1961–1962), p. 199.

from the throne and seats *herself* upon it. It follows from this interpretation that Inanna's intention must, from the first, have been possession of her sister's kingdom. If the centre of the story were really a struggle between the sisters, then it gains probability from a recently translated fragment from Ur. There are fifteen lines of badly mutilated and barely intelligible text, followed by a colophon that states quite unambiguously that this is the final extract of the poem which began *Angalta kigalshē*: 'From the "Great Above"' or 'from "the summits of heaven".' Kramer's translation of the last eight lines of verse, as far as the sense can be made out, is given on p. 165 and lines fourteen and fifteen, the last lines of all,

> kū-eresh-ki-gal-la-ke
> zā-sal-zu-dūg-ga-ām
>
> O Ereshkigal
> Good is your praise!

tell us that the whole poem was made in honour of the Queen of Hell and not of Inanna. Inanna has failed and Ereshkigal triumphed: 'For thou, Persephone, art stronger far'; Aphrodite admits the same in Bion's lament. All the same a change *has* taken place, and the earth will never be the same again because of what Inanna has done. The rhythm of the seasons is secured with the birth of lambs, the time of abundant milk, the shooting of grain and the quick-following harvest, contrasted with the long drought of summer. The beginning of the same fragment of text seems to tell us that in the search for the dead Dumuzi, when his mother and wife have failed to reach him, his sister Geshtinanna succeeds. Something is decreed by Inanna and the year is divided between Dumuzi and Geshtinanna, each passing six months as Ereshkigal's prisoner in the underworld. Thorkild Jacobsen finds the same scenario in the liturgies with the mother of Dumuzi (or Damu) wailing for him in the desert, in the sea of rushes, and at last turning back despairing from 'the river which has no water'. His sister in the end reaches him and he boards the boat which is to bring him up to earth again. As it approaches the upper world a cry rings out ahead to warn the living of the approach of the dead. This brings us to the problem of the death and resurrection of Dumuzi, for though it is certain that he dies, we know nothing at all about his rebirth. The wedding songs celebrate a springtime marriage between Dumuzi and Inanna; the lamentations follow at midsummer when Dumuzi, like his successor Tammuz, is mourned year by year, and now, in Jacobsen's words, 'the god is far away in the Nether World and the dry season with its growing threat of death drags on from day to day'.

A damaged poem concerning Dumuzi and Geshtinanna gives a rather similar story.[7] Geshtinanna is mourning and searching for her brother who calls to her from the Underworld and tells her he is starving for lack of food and drink. She decides to sail down with water and food to find him, and with the boatmen she approaches (or sails by?) the 'Mouth of Heaven' and the 'Mouth of Earth'. Then the text peters out; but the sun-god appears to be concerned with Dumuzi's return, and from other texts we may surmise that when he sails back Geshtinanna remains in his place for her half of the year. These new texts give us what we did not have before: the manner of Dumuzi's return to earth in order to woo the goddess once more, consummate a marriage once more and die once more. Perhaps *Inanna's Journey to Hell* is a commentary on the seasonal liturgies of death and rebirth seen *through the eyes of the dead*. An All Souls' Night is celebrated and death's mystery explained to the living. The mystery is that of the seed that dies to live again: 'except a grain of wheat fall into the earth and die, it abideth by itself alone; but if it die, it beareth much fruit'. The

7. C. J. Gadd and S. N. Kramer in *Ur: Excavation Texts*, VI (1963), pp. 2–5; for Thorkild Jacobsen, see Note on sources (below, p. 132).

drying up of milk in the flocks and the ageing of living things, the slaughter of lambs in the hot season, are all necessary stages of the year's cycle. Or perhaps it does no more than try to answer simple questions: why is it not always springtime? Why is there not always life and green growth? What is the meaning of sorrow and death? Whatever the reason for this journey, it has been made countless times through the centuries; as myth it is always valid, in Homer, in Dante, in Virgil, in the ultimate west with Fursa and Adamnān, and in the waste lands, the *Huis Clos* of the twentieth century.

What then of the songs – the liturgies?

> Far away my son, my Damu gone,
> he cannot come, I weep my child
> far, far away, gone gone, and cannot come,
> and I must weep for him, my own,
> anointed for his death.
> Down by the sacred cedar
> where once I bore my son,
> I, his mother . . .

This surely is neither obscure nor remote any more than Proserpine's loss when she,

> . . . cost Ceres all that pain
> To seek her through the world.

or the girl who sings, 'She is far from the land where her young hero lies'. The love and sacrifice of the sister for her brother, the enormity of loss and dereliction suffered by the mother – these I think do really touch our experience with a certain emotion.

IV

The greater part of the text of *Inanna's Journey* comes from tablets found at Nippur, and now divided between the Museum of the Ancient Orient at Istanbul and the University Museum, Philadelphia; they are to some extent duplicated and also supplemented by tablets found at Ur by Leonard Woolley and now in the British Museum. The Nippur texts, with some 224 legible lines, take the story up to Inanna's confrontation with her husband after her return from hell (line 340). Before this, however, there was until recently a gap immediately after her death in the underworld. This gap of some forty lines has been filled from a patchwork of fragments. Then an important tablet in the Yale Babylonian collection, with its last thirty lines, takes the story from Inanna's confrontation with Dumuzi up to his first prayer to Utu. Dumuzi's flight exists in at least two partly overlapping but partly contrary versions. A recently translated tablet from Ur (UET VI, 11) describes in seventy-two lines what appears to be a second attack on Inanna by the *galle* devils, their capture of Dumuzi (a second time?), his appeal to Utu who changes him into a *sag-kal* snake, his flight to Geshtinanna, the flight continued as the devils arrive at her home, Geshtinanna's refusal to tell them where her brother is and their attack on her, until finally they leave her and go to Dumuzi's 'holy sheepfold' where they seize him again and probably carry him away, because the last lines describe Geshtinanna mourning her brother. The alternative version of the pursuit and capture is for the most part even more difficult. There are 240 lines of text which have been variously interpreted by S. N. Kramer and T. Jacobsen. They begin with the poem describing Dumuzi's dream, part of which had been known for a long time. Since the dream foretells, in allegorical language, what is described as actually taking place in some of the fragments of the first version, I have introduced it into our (Nippur) text after line 359 where a gap occurs. After the dream we continue with the new text from Ur (UET, VI, 11), which I have interrupted at line 66 to insert the fragment describing the final destruction of the sheepfold, and resumed it, using the last five lines as a bridge and introduction to the mourning songs.

There are doubtful places where the different texts join or overlap, so that the total number of lines of the original composition is still uncertain. Some 389 lines have been fitted together using all the known fragments, but allowing for missing lines and variations of text there may have been a total of 426 or even around 500 lines; for it is possible that the Ur version was longer than the Nippur version. The mutilated text (UET, VI, 10), which has on its reverse side the last fifteen lines of the myth, had originally on its obverse 174 lines duplicating the story from the conversation of the Kurgarru and Kalaturru with Ereshkigal, up to the point where Dumuzi is dragged away by the *galle* devils.

The larger part of the text is published in transliteration and translation by S. N. Kramer in the *Journal of Cuneiform Studies*, 4 (1950), 199, and 5 (1951), 1–17, the translation alone in *Ancient Near Eastern Texts Relating to the Old Testament*, ed. E. Pritchard, 1965, pp. 52–7, and partly in S. N. Kramer, *History Begins at Sumer*, 1956, 1961, p. 230. The recently translated Ur texts appear transliterated with translation in *Proceedings of the American Philosophical Society*, 107 (1963), 492 and 510, where they are preceded by a number of marriage and courtship songs and an article by S. N. Kramer, op. cit., p. 485. The mourning songs have been studied especially by Thorkild Jacobsen; 'Dumuzi's Dream' was translated into English by Jacobsen in W. Oppenheim's 'The Interpretation of Dreams', *Transactions of the American Philosophical Society*

(1956), p. 246. A controversial second version of Dumuzi's pursuit, to which the Dream forms an introduction is in the *Journal of Near Eastern Studies*, 12 (1953), p. 160, and see Kramer in *Iraq* 22 (1960), 68, n. 24 etc. For the laments some are given by Thorkild Jacobsen in *Proceedings of the American Philosophical Society*, 107 (1963), p. 473; also 'Toward the Image of Tammuz', *History of Religions*, I (1961), pp. 199 and 208–9, and *Religions in Antiquity*, ed. J. Neusner, Dartmouth College, N.H. 1966, 28 f., which also has a number of marriage songs. In all these publications the major translations are due to Professor Kramer, and his years of work on the texts have provided us with nearly all the available material. A. Falkenstein has given some alternative readings and interpretations in *Bibliotheca Orientalis* 22 (1965), p. 279. in which he is confident both as to Inanna's motive for her journey, and the division of the year in the underworld between Dumuzi and Geshtinanna. I have also made use of the article by A. L. Oppenheim in *Orientalia*, N.S. 19 (1950), p. 129.

INANNA'S JOURNEY TO HELL

I

Inanna in the Underworld

From the summits of heaven
    she looked into the pit,
she was a god on the summits of heaven
    but her heart was in hell,
O Inanna, on the summits,
    your heart in hell!

This lady left earth and heaven
    and went down into the pit,
power and titles she left,
    she went down into the pit,
left Emushkalamma in Badtibira,
    she went down into the pit,
left Zabalam in Giguna,
    she went down into the pit;
Esharra she left in Adab,
    she went down into the pit;

She left in Nippur, Baratushgarra,
    she went down into hell,
she left in Kish, Hursagkalamma,
    she went down into hell,
Eulmash she left in Agade
    down to hell she walked away.

She took the signs in her hands,
put the sandals on her feet,
the seven insignia: she set on her head
the Shugurra, the desert crown,
over her forehead arranged the wig,
she held in her hands the measuring rod
lapis lazuli dark, and the line,
and round her neck she bound
small lapis lazuli gems.
Two stones, perfect ovals, lay on her breast,
a golden ring was gripped in her hand,
the pectoral gems that dazzle men were bound
on her breast, she shadowed her eyes
with bewitching kohl, and over her body
she drew the Pala, robe of sovereignty;
and so Inanna walked away down to hell.

Her minister walked beside her, and now
Inanna speaks to him, Ninshubar,

> 'My loyal minister, angel of eloquence
>   who tells the truth,
> I am on my way, the way to hell,
>   but when I have gone
> you must raise a shout in heaven
>   for my sake,
> a howl in the halls of the gods;
> beat a drum in the holy shrine
>   for my sake,
> scratch your eyes and lacerate your mouth,
> put on a ragged shirt and be a beggar
>   for my sake;
> Then all alone you must go
> to the Bright House of the Mountain,

Enlil's home in Nippur, inside the temple
    cry to Enlil,
"Father, do not let your daughter
    die in hell,
do not let the dust of hell
    bury your bright metal,
nor the lovely lapis lazuli
    be ground into rubble
by the stone-breaker,
    nor the sound
box-wood be lath
    for the carpenter.
Do not let the young girl Inanna
    die in hell."

But if Enlil will not listen,
    go to Ur, weep
in the temple of Nanna, Ekishnugal,
    "Father Nanna,
Do not let your daughter
    die in hell,
Do not let the dust of hell
    bury your bright metal,
nor the lovely lapis lazuli
    be ground into rubble
by the stone-breaker,
    nor the sound
box-wood be lath
    for the carpenter;
Do not let the young girl Inanna
    die in hell."

But if Nanna will not listen
    go to Eridu, weep

in the house of Enki,
    "Father Enki,
Do not let your daughter
    die in hell
Do not let the dust of hell
    bury your bright metal,
nor the lovely lapis lazuli
    be ground into rubble
by the stone-breaker,
    nor the sound
box-wood be lath
    for the carpenter
Do not let the young girl Inanna
    die in hell."

'Father Enki, he is wiser than all the gods,
he knows where the bread is, and the water of life;
at the end he will redeem my life.'

Inanna walks away down to hell,
she had told Ninshubar her minister,
  'What I have said do not forget but do it.'

When Inanna had reached the lapis lazuli halls of hell,
at the gate of hell she sinned, in the halls of hell
she lied,
    'Open the house, Keeper of the door!
    Open the house, open the house, Neti,
    Open the house! I desire to enter,
    I am alone.'
    'Who are you then?'
    'Inanna, come down from the point of dawn.'
    'If you are this Inanna, and from the dawn,
    why have you come to the Land-of-No-Return?

What makes you take the road
from which no traveller goes back?'
and Inanna, the holy one, answers,
    'For my elder sister, for Ereshkigal,
    because of her lord, Gugalanna, who was killed,
    I have come for the last rites.
    This is true.'
and Neti, hell-porter, answers holy Inanna,
    'You must wait Inanna,
    I will speak to the Queen,
    I will speak to Ereshkigal
    the Great Queen of the dark world.'
Then Neti, the chief keeper of the gate of hell,
went into the palace of the Queen Ereshkigal,
he said,
    'My lady, a young girl like one of the gods
    stands at the gate, she wears the signs,
    the sandals and the seven insignia;
    she has set on her head
    Shugurra, the desert crown,
    over her forehead arranged the wig,
    she holds in her hands the measuring rod
    lapis lazuli dark, and the line,
    and round her neck she has bound
    small lapis lazuli gems.

    Two stones, perfect ovals, lie on her breast,
    a golden ring is gripped in her hand,
    the pectoral gems that dazzle men are bound
    on her breast; she has shadowed her eyes
    with bewitching kohl, and over her body
    she has drawn the Pala, robe of sovereignty.'
Then great Ereshkigal answered Neti, the chief
    gate-keeper,
    'Neti, take care, Keeper of the Gate of Hell,

observe what I command. Open the locks
of the seven doors, and at every door enforce
its particular law, from the first
looming of the Dark City.'
Neti the door-keeper bowed; he obeyed the Queen's
  command,
he turned the locks of the seven doors of hell.
At Ganzir, the first looming of the Dark City,
he recited its peculiar law,
    'Go in, Inanna.'
When she had gone he took from her head
Shugurra, the desert crown,
    'Why do you do this?'
                  'Quiet, Inanna,
    this is the law of the underworld
    which must be fulfilled.
    Do not question the rites of hell.'
At the second door when Inanna went in he took
the rod, lapis lazuli dark, and the line,
    'Why do you do this?'
                  'Quiet, Inanna,
    This is the law of the underworld
    which must be fulfilled.
    Do not question the rites of hell.'
At the third door the small
lapis lazuli gems were stripp'd from her throat,
    'Why do you do this?'
                  'Quiet, Inanna,
    this is the law of the underworld
    which must be fulfilled.
    Do not question the rites of hell.'
At the fourth door the two stones, perfect ovals,
that lay on her breast, were taken,
    'Why do you do this?'

'Quiet, Inanna,
this is the law of the underworld
which must be fulfilled.
Do not question the rites of hell.'
At the fifth door the golden ring
gripped in her hand was taken away,
'Why do you do this?'
'Quiet, Inanna,
this is the law of the underworld
which must be fulfilled.
Do not question the rites of hell.'
At the sixth door the pectoral gems
that dazzle men were taken away,
'Why do you do this?'
'Quiet, Inanna,
this is the law of the underworld
which must be fulfilled.
Do not question the rites of hell.'
At the seventh door the Pala was taken, the robe
of sovereignty that covered her body,
'Why do you do this?'
'Quiet, Inanna,
this is the law of the underworld
which must be fulfilled.
Do not question the rites of hell.'

Naked Inanna dropped on her knees
for great Ereshkigal had mounted the throne.
In her presence the Seven Judges pronounced
    the sentence,
they fastened their eyes on her,
    eyes of death,
they spoke the sentence
    of the accused,

they uttered the cry
      of the accursed.
Inanna instantly sickened
      to death,
her body was a corpse that hung
      on a spike.

After three days and nights Ninshubar,
the loyal minister, angel of eloquence who tells
the truth, Ninshubar raised a shout through heaven
      for her sake,
a howl in the halls of the gods;
beat a drum in the holy shrine
      for her sake,
scratched his eyes and lacerated his mouth,
put on a ragged shirt and was a beggar
      for her sake.
Then all alone he went
to the Bright House of the Mountain,
to Enlil's home in Nippur, inside the house,
      he cried to Enlil,

            'Father Enlil,
      Do not let your daughter
            die in hell,
      do not let the dust of hell
            bury your bright metal,
      nor the lovely lapis lazuli
            be ground into rubble
      by the stone-breaker,
            nor the sound
      box-wood be lath
            for the carpenter.

Do not let the young girl Inanna
    die in hell.'
Father Enlil answered Ninshubar,

    'My daughter is insatiable,
    she brought it on herself,
    when she performed the rites
    of hell; now she must bear the law
    of the underworld.'

So Enlil would not listen. In Ur
    in Ekishnugal
in Nanna's temple weeping
    he cried to Nanna,
                'Father,
Do not let your daughter
    die in hell,
do not let the dust of hell
    bury your bright metal,
nor the lovely lapis lazuli
    be ground into rubble
by the stone-breaker,
    nor the sound
box-wood be lath
    for the carpenter.
Do not let the young girl Inanna
    die in hell.'
Father Nanna answered Ninshubar,

    'My daughter is insatiable,
    she brought it on herself,
    when she performed the rites
    of hell; now she must bear the law
    of the underworld.'

And Nanna would not listen.
Ninshubar travelled to Eridu,

inside the house he called to Enki
weeping,
    'Father Enki,
Do not let your daughter
    die in hell,
do not let the dust of hell
    bury your bright metal,
nor the lovely lapis lazuli
    be ground into rubble
by the stone-breaker,
    nor the sound
box-wood be lath
    for the carpenter.
Do not let the young girl Inanna
    die in hell.'
Father Enki answered Ninshubar,
    'What has happened to my daughter?
        I am grieved.
    What has happened to Inanna?
        So much grief.
    What has happened to the Queen of all the Earth?
        I am grieved.
    What has happened to the beloved of heaven?
        So much grief.'

Enki took dirt from his finger-nail and formed the Kurgarru,
dirt from his red-lacquered finger-nail and formed Kalaturru.
To Kurgarru he gave the food of life,
to Kalaturru he gave the water of life;
to Kurgarru and Kalaturru Enki said,
    'Turn your footsteps down to hell,
    buzz round the gate like flies,
    circle the pivot. She is sick,
    mother Ereshkigal is in labour

with her children. No sheet
covers her body, her holy breast
is naked as a pitcher,
[a thing] of copper beside her;
the hair on her head is leek-dyed
black. She will moan,
"My entrails, O my entrails."
Say to her, "Our Queen moans,
'My entrails, O my entrails.'"
She will moan,
"My presence, O my presence."
Say to her, "Our Queen moans,
'My presence, O my presence.'"
She will say, "Who speaks to me?
Who calls to my entrails from theirs?
from my presence to theirs?
If you are gods I bless you,
if mortals I give you good luck,
Only swear by heaven and earth."

'They will offer water from the river,
do not take the water of death.
They will give you grain from the fields
of the dead, do not take that seed,
only say to her,
      "Give us the corpse
that hangs on a spike."
Over the corpse one of you scatter
the food of life, and the other sprinkle
the living water and then Inanna will stand up.'

Kalaturru and Kurgarru did as Enki said,
they turned their footsteps down to hell,
buzzed like flies round the gate,

circled the pivot; while she lay sick,
mother Ereshkigal was in labour
with her children. No sheet
covered her body, her holy breast
was naked as a pitcher,
[a thing] of copper beside her;
the hair on her head was leek-dyed
black. When she moaned
    'My entrails, O my entrails,'
they said to her,
     'Our Queen moans,
     "my entrails, O my entrails."'
When she moaned,
    'My presence, O my presence,'
they said to her,
     'Our Queen moans,
     "My presence, O my presence.
     Who speaks to me?
     Who calls to my entrails from theirs?
     from my presence to theirs?
     If you are gods I bless you,
     if mortals I give you good luck,
     Only swear by heaven and earth."'

They swore by heaven and earth;
they were offered the water of the river,
but they did not take the water of death.
They were given grain from the fields of the
   dead,
but they did not take the seed;
They said,
    'Give us the corpse that hangs on a spike.'
Ereshkigal answered,
    'Behold your Queen!'

'If this is our Queen, give us this corpse.'
It was given them.

Over the corpse hanging on a spike
they scattered the bread of life,
they sprinkled the living water,
and Inanna stood up alive.
She will come from the pit, but the Anunnaki
seized her, the Judges said,
    'Who has ever returned out of hell unharmed?
    To escape the pit alive she must leave
    another who shall wait in her place.'

II

Inanna's Return from Hell

She is coming, Inanna is coming
from the pit! Devils are fastened
to her thighs, devils walk beside her,
meagre like reeds, thin as pikestaves.
There goes in front of her a thing
with a sceptre, but he is no minister.
One walks beside her wearing his weapon
on his hip, but this is no fighting man.
These that hug her, these beside her
are things that neither eat nor drink,
things not appeased with sprinkled flour,
who do not drink the holy water;
they snatch a wife from her husband's loins,
and a child from the nurse's nipple.
She is coming, Inanna is coming
from the pit!

Now that Inanna is home from hell
Ninshubar lies at her feet,
he lies in the dirt, and the devils say
to holy Inanna,
　　　　　'Inanna,
　　here you must wait,
　　at this city; this one
　　we will carry off.'
But holy Inanna answers,
　　'This is my loyal minister, my angel of eloquence
　　who tells the truth, he did not fail me nor forget
　　my words;
　　He raised a shout in heaven
　　　　for my sake,
　　a howl in the halls of the gods;
　　beat a drum in the holy shrine
　　　　for my sake,
　　scratched his eyes, lacerated his mouth,
　　put on a ragged shirt and was a beggar
　　　　for my sake.
　　All alone he went
　　to the Bright House of the Mountain,
　　Enlil's home in Nippur, in Ur
　　to the house of Nanna, in Eridu
　　to the house of Enki,
　　　　He saved my life.'
　　'Let's go with her then to Umma,
　　to the temple Sigkurshagga.
　　Let's go with her.'
In Sigkurshagga in Umma
Shara lies at her feet,
lies in the dirt in rags
and the devils said,
to holy Inanna,

148

'Inanna,
here you must wait,
at this city; this one
we will carry away.'
Inanna answers,
'Because he wore rags
and lay in the dirt
on no account
shall you carry him off.'
'To Emushkalamma in Badtibira
to the temple let's go with her.'
From Emushkalamma in Badtibira
Latarak lies at her feet in rags,
'Inanna,
here you must wait,
at this city; this one
we will carry away.'
Inanna, the holy one, answered,
'Latarak
is my right-hand man,
my Captain; on no account
shall you carry him off.'
But in Kullab the young shepherd,
Dumuzi, put on a beautiful robe,
he mounted the throne high up above,
and the seven devils gripped his thighs
like mortal sickness.
The flute-song of the shepherd
is broken, the pipes are shattered
in front of him,
for on him Inanna has fastened
the eyes of death,
she has spoken the sentence
of the accused,

she has uttered the cry
>of the accursed,
>>'As for that one, carry him off!'

This was how holy Inanna gave up her shepherd
into the power of the devils.

III

The Pursuit of Dumuzi

Those that went with him,
those that went with Dumuzi
were things that neither eat,
nor drink water, things
not appeased with sprinkled flour,
nor the holy water of libations.
They bring to a woman's body
no sweet satiety,
nor fondle the happy children,
but they snatch a boy from his father's knee
and the son's wife from her husband's house.

Dumuzi wept, his face was livid,
he held up his hands to the sun
in heaven, and he said,
>'Utu, you are the brother of my wife, Inanna,
>I am your sister's husband,
>Who brings the cream to your mother's house?
>Is it not I? Who brings milk
>to Ningal's house? It is I.
>Change me, transform my body

into a snake, and take my hands and feet away.
Transform me so that my devils
will not hold me, transform me
and I shall escape.'

Utu received his tears, changed his body
and Dumuzi escaped.

Dumuzi's Bad Dream

His heart was full,
he went into the barren land and wept;
the shepherd's heart was full,
out in the barren land he wept.

His flute hung from his neck,
he cried with the cry of the lost,
'Weep, weep, wilderness weep,
O fields lament, weep, O weep.
Out among the river crabs
weep for me, O weep;
out among the river frogs
weep for me, weep.
Mother cry aloud, cry for me,
Sirtur cry aloud.
O my mother, she has not ten loaves,
let her cry aloud,
my mother has not five loaves,
crying aloud.
On the day I die
she is bereft,
in the barren lands like my mother
my eyes weep,

weep like my sister,
    my little sister.'

He has lain himself down,
    wind in the south,
the shepherd lies sleeping,
    wind in the south,
the shepherd lies dreaming,
    the wind was in the south.
Out of his dream suddenly awake the shepherd
    leaping up
Dumuzi rubs his eyes,
    he stands bemused.

    'Bring me my sister, my Geshtinanna,
        she understands letters,
    bring my little sister, my scribe,
        she is the singer
    who understands the song,
        bring me my sister.
    Bring my wise girl,
        she can read visions,
    bring me my sister, bring me
        the little one, she understands
    the heart of the whole matter,
        O my sister!
    Bring me my sister, I shall tell her
        all my dream.

    Little sister, you wise interpreter,
        in this dream, rushes shot up.
            It was for me they shot.
    A single reed stood alone,
        its head shook.

For me it shook.
Two reeds together
and one was taken,
For me it was taken.
A tall tree overturned,
alone in the wood.
For me overturned.
Water was spilled
on to my swept hearth.
It spilled for me.
Tipped from its stand
my scoured churn.
Tipped for me.
My clean mug that hangs on a peg,
dropped from the peg.
Dropped for me.
My crook was lost,
the owl's claw and the falcon.
[What does it hold?]
The goat and kids
lie stretched in the dust,
their mouths are blue.
With broken forelegs the ram
paws at the ground,
paws it for me.
The churn overturned
and no milk flowing,
The mug on its side
not for my drinking,
Dumuzi's sheepfold
to the wind wide open.'

'Brother, this dream is bad,
it cannot be erased.

Dumuzi, your dream is bad,
    it cannot be erased.
Rushes and reeds sprang up,
    they sprang for you.
        Evil springs out on you.
A single reed alone,
    shaking its head,
        shaking for you.
Your mother is rocking her head,
    rocking for you.
Two reeds together,
    you and I, brother,
one of us two
    will be taken.
The tall tree overturned
    alone in the wood,
evil overtakes you
    in the reeds alone.
Water spilled over
    your swept hearth.
        For you it is spilled.
Your scoured churn
    tipped from its stand.
        Tipped for you.
Fallen from the peg
    your clean mug.
        Fallen for you.
From your mother's lap
    you have fallen down.
Your crook gone.
    [You must go too.]
What the owl and falcon
    hold in their claws
        [Evil befalls!]

Your goats and kids
    stretched out in the dust,
        their mouths are blue.
With broken forelegs your ram
    paws at the ground.
        Paws it for you.'

Little devils are chattering to great ones,
    'Come on, we'll go to Inanna,
    we'll sit in her lap so holy-O.'

The devils went in to Uruk,
they seized Inanna, the holy one.

    'Come away down, Inanna,
    down to the great Dark City,
    there where your wilful heart took you,
    down into hell, down
    to the home of Ereshkigal,
    come away down, Inanna.
    But, Inanna, you are not to put on
    your beautiful dress,
    the *Ma*-dress, *Pala*-dress,
    the dress of your sovereignty,
    come away, come away down Inanna.
    Take off your crown, Inanna,
    of the holy salutation,
    come away, come away down.
    Do not make up your face,
    not now Inanna,

but come away down to the underworld,
come away down to hell.'

They held on fast to holy Inanna
and stricken with terror she gave Dumuzi
into the power of the devils.
They said,
    'This boy, put fetters on his feet,
    truss him up, pinion his neck in stocks.'

They flew at his face with hooks and bits
and bodkins, they slashed his body with a heavy axe,
they made him stand and made him squat;
they pinioned that boy by the arms
and covered his face with a mask
of agony; he held up his hands
to the sun in heaven:
    'Utu, Utu, I am your friend,
    I married your sister,
    I am someone you know.
    She went away down to the pit and all
    for that she has given me over,
    me in her place in hell to sojourn.
    Utu, just judge that you are,
    do not let them take me away!
    Transform my body, take away my hands,
    save me from out of the power of my devils
    and never let them find me.
    I will glide through the upland meadows
    like a *sag-kal* snake and escape
    with my soul to her home, to my sister
    Geshtinanna.'
Utu received his tears, changed his body,
took away his hands, and Dumuzi glided

through the uplands like a *sag-kal* snake;
his soul plunged with the falcon's stoop
that follows a sparrow, he carried it straight
to the home of Geshtinanna.

Geshtinanna gazed at her brother, then
she tore her cheeks and lacerated her mouth,
she dropped her head on her knees,
ripped up her dress for the agony
of the boy; she let out her cry
of desolation,

       'O Brother,
so few, so few days now
brother, O shepherd, O Ama-ushamgal-anna,
how few days more brother, O brother.
Now, no more, you have no wife,
no child nor any companion,
now, no more. You are the boy
who brings little delight
to his mother, my brother, O
my brother.'

The devils had discovered Dumuzi
and now they surround him, little devils
chatter to great ones,

       'Dumuzi,
we are *your* devils,
we have no father, no sister,
no wife, no brother, but over
the skies and earth we hover,
watchdogs and spies;
we are *your* devils, Dumuzi;
we hug a man's sides,
we know no compassion,

evil and good are equal,
we are impartial.

Whoever saw anyone terrified so?
His soul won't rest in peace very long.
Don't go to his friend's home,
not to the home of his wife's brother,
but search for the shepherd at the home of Geshtinanna.'

They clapped their hands with cries which never
stopped pouring from their mouths.
In search of Dumuzi devils
went to the home of Geshtinanna.
They shouted at her,
    'Show us your brother!'
But where he was she would not tell them.
They choked her,
they buried her in earth,
    but she told them nothing.
They covered her in earth,
they lacerated her body,
    but she told them nothing.
They choked her,
they ripped her clothes,
    but she told them nothing.
They tipped pitch into her lap,
    but she told them nothing.
They did not find Dumuzi
    in the house of Geshtinanna.
Little devils chattering
to great ones,
    'Let's go to the sacred sheep-fold.'
It was then that the seven
devils entered the shippon.

When the first went in
the swept hearth was spoiled.

When the second went in
milk turned sour.

When the third went in
water was fouled.

When the fourth went in
the shippon was empty.

When the fifth went in
dust smothered it.

When the sixth went into the fold
he tipped all the tackle over.

The sheepfold was desolate while Dumuzi
like a young strong man slept on.

But the devils raised a howl,
with chatterings they filled the fold,

while the noble husband of the Queen
of Heaven was sleeping.

They howled through the sheep-fold,
they told the young king,
    'Your grazing flocks
    have been driven away;
    though you are the husband
    of Inanna, our lady,
    the son of the goddess,
    the hurricane has carried them away.

Young prince, young brother,
the hurricane tears you away.
Your work is ended, your crown
tumbled, your beautiful robes,
sceptre and sandals.
The lord must leave his sheep-fold
and never return, never . . .'

By the sacred shippon devils seize Dumuzi,
they surround him now they have got him;
they seize and stare him down. They go at him
with axes, slashing his thighs with knives,
they press in close around him.

On account of her brother she wandered through the city,
the sister Geshtinanna, like a bird complaining,
　'Brother, let me come
　where evil befell you.'

IV

Dumuzi Mourned

Who is your sister? I am she.
Who is your mother? I am she.
Day dawns the same for you and me.
This is the same day we shall see.

The Wife's Song

The wild bull lives no more,
he is stretched out on the ground,
    he lives no more.
So fast asleep, wild bull?
How deep the ewe sleeps
and the lamb, how deep,
    and the wild bull sleeps.
How deep the goat sleeps
and the kid, how deep,
    and the wild bull sleeps.
I will call the hills and valleys,
I will call the hill of the bison,
'Where is the young man
    my husband?
It is useless to bring him food,
    where is he now?
It is useless to bring him drink,
    where is he now
and my lovely girls and lads?'

'The bison has carried him away to the mountains,
the bison has carried away the young man, your husband.'
Mountain bison with flecked eyes,
Mountain bison with crushing teeth,
Ah bison!

His sleep is silent,
this sleep of his
    it is a silent sleep.
This is one to whom

it is useless to bring food,
useless to bring drink,
        his sleep is silent.
My lovely girls and lads
are all asleep,
        silently sleeping.

He is dead and has left me,
my husband! He died
at the hands of your people,
my young man has left me.
For me in the night he will never again
unhitch the catch of his clothing.
        My husband.
The jackal lies in your bed,
the raven broods in your sheepfold,
only the wind plays the shepherd's pipe,
only the north wind sings your song.
        My husband.

The Song of the Pipe

Hark the piping!
My heart is piping in the wilderness
        an instrument of grief.
'Though I am queen in love's own temple,
        and shatter mountains.'
'Though I am Ninsun, the mother of my lord.'
'And I Geshtinanna, the vine of heaven,
        the daughter – what does it matter?'
My heart is piping grief for him
in the wilderness,

piping where the young man used to live,
piping where Dumuzi pitched in the desert
once upon a time, on Shepherd's Hill.

The Mother Sings

Hark the piping!
My heart is piping in the wilderness
where the young man once went free.
He is a prisoner now in death's kingdom,
    lies bound where once he lived.
The ewe gives up her lamb
and the nanny-goat her kid.
My heart is piping in the wilderness
    an instrument of grief.
Now she is coming to death's kingdom,
she is the mother desolate
in a desolate place; where once
he was alive, now he lies
like a young bull felled to the ground.
Into his face she stares, seeing
what she has lost – his mother
who has lost him to death's kingdom.
O the agony she bears,
shuddering in the wilderness,
she is the mother suffering so much.
    'It is you,'
she cried to him,
    'but you are changed.'
The agony, the agony she bears.
Woe to the house and the inner room.

The Son's Reply

There can be no answer
  to her desolate calling,
it is echoed in the wilderness,
  for I cannot answer.
Though the grass will shoot
  from the land
I am not grass, I cannot come
  to her calling.
The waters rise for her,
I am not water to come
  for her wailing,
I am not shoots of grass
  in a dead land.

[*Neither Dumuzi's wife nor his mother can reach him; but it seems as though his sister succeeds in boarding a boat and descending to hell, where they change places, and Dumuzi returns to the world of the living. But first, a cry is heard ahead of the boat, warning all the living of the approach of the dead.*]

City of Ur! Lock up! Lock up!
At my loud cry
lock up your houses,
lock up your temples,
City of Ur! Lock up!
Tell the young bride of the temple
she must abandon her house.
City, lock up! Lock up!

INANNA'S JOURNEY TO HELL

Postscript: A fragment of the end

My young man has gone,
half the year, you, Dumuzi,
for half the year,
for half the year your sister.
On the day of your desire,
on that very day you shall depart.
On the day your sister shall desire it,
on her day she shall come,
they shall return with Dumuzi at their head
where Inanna has put him.

O ERESHKIGAL, GREAT IS YOUR PRAISE!

Introduction to Adapa: the Man

THE name is not 'a man' but 'man', it is Adam; but the story of this Adam is of fooling and paradox. Unlike Utnapishtim, the Babylonian Noah who won eternal life for himself through obedience to a god, in Adapa mankind was given the chance of eternal life and lost it through obedience to a god. The scene of the beginning is Eridu, in southern Mesopotamia. One of the oldest Sumerian cities, it stood on the edge of a great lagoon near the Persian Gulf and was sacred to Ea, the Sumerian Enki. The father of the gods, Anu, is still in this story the supreme authority in heaven. Of the two lesser gods, Tammuz and Gizzida, who stand at the East Gate of heaven, Tammuz has descended from Dumuzi, and Gizzida was a god of healing sometimes also connected with the Underworld. Gizzida was called Lord of the Tree of Truth, as Dumuzi–Tammuz was Lord of the Tree of Life – trees that were stars planted in heaven. Besides Anu's messenger or minister and the South Wind, these are the only protagonists.

The text is put together from three fragments; the oldest and longest was found in Egypt among the fourteenth-century archives, mostly diplomatic correspondence, of Tell el Amarna. The two shorter fragments were in Ashurbanipal's library at Nineveh. The el Amarna text has no metrical form, it is (presumably) prose; and the story (the sting in the tail notwith-standing) is nearest to a morality or *conte*. The morality cuts more than one way, and it is worth noticing that for one split second, before his ignominious return to earth, Adapa is allowed the vision of heaven. Though every kind of trouble lies ahead, this is something that belongs to Adapa; the vision cannot be taken away from man.

ADAPA: THE MAN

In those days, in those years long ago at Eridu, the city which stands on a sweet lagoon, there was a man. He was wise like one of the gods. When he gave an order it was as though Ea, the master himself, that subtle god, had spoken; for Ea is the master of subtlety, and he also controls the waters. Ea had made him a leader, a man to be followed. He gave him sagacity and intelligence enough to comprehend the design of the world: but he made him a dying man.

In those days, in those years, he was man's first pattern, scrupulous in his service to the temple, one with clean hands; the sage of Eridu was accounted wise even among the Great Gods. No one questioned his orders. Daily he stocked up the city with bread and drinking water, baking bread with the bakers of Eridu, steering the ship that fished for Eridu, going through the ritual with clean hands. Only *he* could set and clear the god's table.

In those days, while Ea lay at ease on his bed and this man Adapa was busy in the sanctuary, the household had need of fresh stores of fish. So Adapa boarded the sailing boat at the quay-side, the one which is sacred to the New Moon. It blew a following wind and he let the boat run before the gale. He steered with the oar, sailing out into the wide sea alone.

In the middle of the sea Adapa went about catching fish; the sea was calm as a mirror. Then the South Wind got up; it capsized him, and he plunged down into the world of fish. In his desperate anger Adapa yelled out a curse,

'South Wind, you rose out of malice, I will break your wing', and as he spoke the wing of the South Wind shattered, and for seven days it did not blow on to the land at all.

Anu, the god who reigns in heaven, called out to his servant Ilabrat,

'Why has the South Wind not blown on to the land for seven days?' Ilabrat answered,

'My Lord, the man, Ea's son, has shattered the wing of the South Wind in his arrogant fashion.'

When he heard this Anu got up angrily from his throne. He sent his messenger to Ea, because he is wise and knows the gods well. They spoke together, and Anu shouted,

'Fetch the man here!'

Ea gave the man a warning, for he knew the ways of heaven. He told him to go in rags and in mourning with his hair uncut and hanging loose.

'You must go up the road to the top of heaven and appear before Anu, the king. When you have reached the gate of heaven you will see two gods, Tammuz and Gizzida, who stand there together. They will ask,

"Man, for whose sake do you look like this?"

Answer,

"Two gods have left our land, I mourn for them."

"What gods are they?"

"I mourn for Tammuz and Gizzida."

'Then they will smile at each other and say kind words to Anu; they will show you his *gracious* face. When you are standing in front of Anu they will offer the bread of death; do not eat it. They will offer the water of death; do not drink it. They will bring a garment; put on the garment; and when they bring oil anoint yourself. Take care that you do not forget this advice. Remember!'

The messenger from Anu came for the man. He led him up the road of the firmament; he approached the East Gate of heaven. Tammuz and Gizzida stood at the gate; when they saw him they said,

'Heavens, Man! Why do you look like this? Whom are you mourning?'

'Two gods have left our land, I mourn for them.'

'What gods are they?'

'Tammuz and Gizzida, I mourn for them.'

They exchanged glances and smiled. Adapa approached the lord of heaven. Anu looked at him and said,

'You, Man, why did you break the wing of the South Wind?' The man answered,

'My lord, I was catching fish in the middle of the sea for the household of my master, Ea. The sea was a mirror but the South Wind got up, he capsized me and I plunged down to the world of fish, and in the anger of my heart I cursed him.'

Then Tammuz and Gizzida, standing beside him, spoke kind words. They soothed the heart of the king of heaven so that he said, speaking to them,

'What was Ea about to give knowledge of all nature to a wretch of a man, to make him like one of us, and with such a name for wisdom? But now that he is here what else can we do? Fetch the bread of life and he shall eat it.'

When they brought him the bread of life he would not eat. When they brought him the water of life he did not drink it. When they brought him a garment he put it on; and when they brought oil he anointed himself.

Then Anu, the lord of heaven, looked at the man and laughed,

'Ah, Adapa, why did you neither eat nor drink, stupid man; perverse mankind; you will never now have eternal life.'

'My master Ea ordered me, "You shall not eat, you shall not drink".'

Loudly Anu laughed again at the doings of Ea,

'Of all the gods of heaven and of earth, as many as there

may be, whoever gave such an order! Who can circumvent the will of Anu?'

Then the man looked from the horizon of heaven to the meridian; he saw the majesty of heaven, and Anu gave the man his orders and he gave to the priests of Eridu the rule of their lives. But as for him, the man child of man, who broke the wing of the South Wind in his arrogant fashion, who went up to heaven – he brought on us the sufferings of mankind. He brought disease to our bodies that only the Lady of Healing can assuage.

May sickness depart. May there be no more disease; but as for him, let him not lie down in gentle sleep again, nor feel the happiness that men know in their hearts.

Note on *A Prayer to the Gods of Night*

AN Old Babylonian prayer of the first half of the second millennium, its source is not known; but the scene is night in any one of the packed sweltering cities of Mesopotamia during the few hours of quiet when nothing seems to stir, and the great stars look exceedingly near.

See F. J. Stephens in *Ancient Near Eastern Texts Relating to the Old Testament*, ed. J. B. Pritchard, 1955, p. 390.

A PRAYER TO THE GODS OF NIGHT

They are lying down, the Great Ones,
the bars have fallen, the bolts are shot,
the crowds and all the people rest,
the open gates are locked.
The gods of the land, the goddesses,
Shamash Sin Adad Ishtar,
sun, moon, turmoil, love
lie down to sleep in heaven.
The judgement seat is empty now,
for no god now is still at work.
Night has drawn down the curtain,
the temples and the sanctuaries are silent, dark.
Now the traveller calls to his god,
defendant and plaintiff sleep in peace,
for the judge of truth, the father of the fatherless,
Shamash, has gone to his chamber.
'O Great Ones, Princes of the Night,
Bright Ones, Gibil the furnace, Irra
war-lord of the Underworld,
Bow-star and Yoke, Orion, Pleiades, Dragon,
the Wild Bull, the Goat, and the Great Bear,
stand by me in my divination.
By this lamb that I am offering,
may truth appear!'

GLOSSARY OF NAMES

THE glossary gives a short explanation of names of gods and other persons and places referred to; it includes the titles of Marduk with which he is addressed in the 'Hymn of the Fifty Names' at the end of *The Babylonian Creation*. These titles are full of ambiguities and puns, and translation gives only an approximate rendering of their meanings; some cannot be translated at all. The principal actors in the various poems, hymns and tales are described more fully in the introductory passages to each, and page references to these descriptions are given at the end of the glossary note. Cross-references are rendered in italics.

Abūba: Or Abūbu, the flood-storm or cloud-burst, a mythical winged being, an ally of *Marduk* in his battle against *Tiamat*.

Adab: An important Sumerian city.

Adad: God of storms, weather-god.

Adapa: 'Man', the hero of an Akkadian tale; see p. 167.

Addu: A form of *Adad*, storm and rain, assimilated to *Marduk* in the 'Hymn of the Fifty Names'.

Agade: See *Akkad*.

Agaku: A composite name that implies wrath and love, also a crown of perfection or a charm; one of the punning titles of *Marduk*, typical of the ambivalence of the gods towards men.

Agilma: A composite name suggesting waves and creation; one of the titles of *Marduk*.

Akkad: Or Agade, an important Mesopotamian city that gave its name to the semitic inhabitants of the land, and to their language; it lies north of the principal Sumerian centres.

Akītu: The festival of the New Year; see p. 44.

Ama-ushamgal-anna: A title of *Dumuzi* translated, 'The Mother, the Dragon of Heaven' (Kramer) or 'The Power in the Date-palm' (Jacobsen).

Anshar: The horizon of the sky, in 'The Babylonian Creation' a male god who with *Kishar* is born from the silt and is parent of *Anu*, heaven; see p. 30.

Anu: Sumerian An, heaven, the sky and the god of the skies, the child of *Anshar* and *Kishar* and the father of *Ea*; see p. 29.

Anunnaki: Also written Anunna; generally the gods of the lower regions; in 'Inanna's Journey to Hell' they are the seven judges of hell, but sometimes they are gods of heaven. In The Babylonian Creation they are the defeated rebel gods who build Marduk's *Babylon*; see p. 31.

Apsū: Sumerian Abzu, 'the abyss', the primeval waters under the earth; see p. 25.

Aranunna: 'Counsellor', one of the titles of *Marduk*.

Asarluhi: A title of supremacy given to *Marduk* by *Anshar*.

Asaru: One of *Marduk*'s titles connecting him with gifts of water and garden irrigation.

Asarualim: 'The gods learn humility before him', one of *Marduk*'s titles.

Asarualim Nunna: The same as *Asarualim* but with added brightness and glory.

Asaruludu: One of two names given to *Marduk* by *Anu*, his grandfather, the other being his usual name, Marduk. It is the seventh title in the 'Hymn of the Fifty Names'; a mysterious name conveying magical powers.

Asharu: *Marduk*'s penultimate title in the 'Hymn of the Fifty Names'.

Babylon: From the second millennium the principal city of southern Mesopotamia; see p. 39.

Badtibira: A city in southern Sumer.

Barashakushu: 'He who rests on the throne', a title of *Marduk*.

Baratushgarra: or Baradurgarra, *Inanna*'s temple in *Nippur*.

Bēl: 'Lord'. *Marduk* is often called Bel-Marduk, or simply Bel, 'The Lord'; the Canaanite 'Baal' is the same word.

Bēl Mātāti: 'Lord of all Lands', *Marduk*'s last title in the 'Hymn of the Fifty Names'.

Bīt Akītu: The temple of the New Year festival; see p. 44.

Damkina: A goddess, the wife of *Ea* and mother of *Marduk* in 'The Babylonian Creation'.

Damu: 'The Child', a young god connected with life-giving waters, sometimes identified with *Dumuzi*.

Dumuduku: Also Marduku, 'the child of Duku', the 'pure' and 'cosmic' mountain, meaning *Enlil*; also a room in Enlil's temple in *Nippur* where destinies were decided, hence transferred to the 'Hall of Destiny' in the temple at Babylon, called the *Ubshukinna*.

Dumūzi: 'The true or faithful son', the shepherd god. Sometimes a title of kings, particularly the king of *Uruk*; see also *Ama-ushamgalanna* and *Tammuz*; and p. 118.

Duranki: 'The bond that unites heaven and earth', an ancient name for *Enlil's* holy city, *Nippur*. It was here that traditionally Enlil split the earth's crust with his pick-axe so that primordial man could break through.

Ea: Sumerian *Enki*, the god of sweet waters and wisdom, a patron of arts, the father of *Marduk*, and one of the creators of mankind to whom he was generally kindly disposed, the chief god of *Eridu*; see p. 31.

Edin: The desert, the waste land, the underworld; see p. 121.

Ekishnugal: The temple of the Moon in *Ur*.

Ekur: 'The bright mountain'; *Enlil's* temple in *Nippur*; see *Dumuduku*.

Emushkalamma: A temple in *Badtibira* in southern Sumer.

Enbilulu: Perhaps connected with wells and irrigation, one of *Marduk's* titles in the 'Hymn of the Fifty Names'.

Enki: 'Lord of the Earth', the Sumerian forerunner of *Ea*; see p. 31.

Enlil: God of the universal air, the chief god of *Nippur*; see p. 33.

Epadun: A title of *Marduk*, similar to *Enbilulu*.

Ereshkigal: 'The Queen of the Great Below', the Queen of Hell and the Dead.

Eridu: A Sumerian city at the head of the Persian Gulf sacred to *Enki-Ea*.

Esagila: In Sumerian 'The raising of the head', the name of *Marduk's* temple in *Babylon*; in 'The Babylonian Creation' it is built for him by the defeated rebel gods.

Esharra: *Inanna's* temple in *Adab*.

Esizkur: 'Belonging to the house of prayer', a title of *Marduk* sometimes understood as referring to the *Bit Akitu* visited on the tenth day of the New Year festival.

Eulmash: A temple in *Agade* (Akkad).

Galla: Or 'Gallē', the little devils, underworld spirits able to operate on earth where they enforce the laws of the underworld and its gods; they pursue fugitives and law-breakers and carry them down to the underworld, and *Dumuzi* they pursue like Erinyes.

Ganzir: A name for the underworld; the meaning is uncertain.

Geshtinanna: 'Lady of the Vine' or 'Vine of Heaven', the sister of *Dumuzi*, she is a singer and has a reputation for learning and so is identified with Bēlit Sēri, the Akkadian form of Nin-Edin, 'The Lady of the Waste Lands' who, in 'The Epic of Gilgamesh', is the scribe and recorder of the underworld.

Gibil: The god of fire, a patron of smiths and metal-workers; it is under this aspect that he is assimilated to *Marduk* in the 'Hymn of the Fifty Names'.

Giguna: A temple grove sacred to *Inanna* in *Zabalam*.

Gil: Refers to things that are high, hence the heaps of grain, one of *Marduk*'s titles in the 'Hymn of the Fifty Names'.

Gilma: Fire, flame, a title of *Marduk*.

Gishnumunab: The virility of the creator god, a title of *Marduk*.

Gizzida: Also Ningizzida, 'Lord of the Tree of Life', a god of fertility and healing, also connected with the underworld; in the *Adapa* myth he is the companion of *Tammuz* with whom he stands guard at the gate of heaven.

Gugal: 'Great abundance and riches', a title of *Marduk*.

Gugalanna: 'Great Bull of Heaven', a title of the husband of *Ereshkigal*; in the poem of 'Inanna's Journey to Hell' he is recently dead.

Hegal: A title of *Marduk*.

Hursagkalamma: *Inanna*'s temple in Kish in northern Sumer.

Igigi: The heavenly gods, sometimes in opposition to the *Anunnaki*, (gods of the underworld); a collective name.

Ilabrat: *Anu*'s messenger and servant in the *Adapa* tale.

Imhullu: 'The evil wind', one of *Marduk*'s allies.

Inanna: The great goddess of *Uruk*; in Sumerian her name means 'Lady of Heaven' from an earlier Nin-an-ah; it is also connected with the date-clusters; she is 'Our Lady of the Granary' and 'of the Byre'; she is the goddess of love and fertility and was later endowed with some of the celestial attributes of the semitic *Ishtar*; her name may be Innin; see p. 118, f.

Irkingu: A title of *Marduk* as conqueror of *Kingu*.

Irra: A storm god.

Ishtar: The semitic goddess of love and war identified with *Inanna*, the planet Venus and, in Syria and Palestine, Astarte, Ashtaroth.

Kaka: Or Gaga, messenger of *Anshar*.

Kalaturrū: Or Kalatur, with *Kurgarru* two sexless beings created by *Enki* to achieve the rescue of *Inanna* from the underworld; also a religious order serving the goddess.

Kingu: This Sumerian name suggests toil, labour; a 'first-born' god and ally of *Tiamat*.

Kinma: A title of *Marduk* as leader of gods.

Kishar: 'The horizon of earth', the female counterpart of *Anshar*.

Kulili: A monster created by *Tiamat*, of uncertain meaning; it has been translated 'dragon-fly' for 'flying dragon' (?) or 'fish-man'.

Kullab: A sacred quarter of *Uruk*.

Kur: Originally the Sumerian for 'mountain', hence 'foreign land' from the mountains surrounding the marshlands and plains of Mesopotamia; it came to mean underworld, the hell of *Ereshkigal*, and even an underworld monster.

Kurgarrū: Or Kurgarra; the companion of *Kalaturru*.

Kusariqu: A monster created by *Tiamat*, sometimes translated 'wild bison' and 'centaur'.

Lahāmu: Silt, the female counterpart of *Lahmu*.

Lahmu: Silt, with *Lahamu* the male half of a pair of primordial beings; see p. 25.

Latarak: The guardian god of the city of *Badtibira*.

Lugal: A Sumerian word meaning 'king' and 'ruler', often added to other names as a prefix.

Lugalabdubur: 'King of the treasure-house' and 'of the firm foundations', a title of *Marduk*.

Lugaldimmerankia: 'King of the gods of heaven and earth', a title of *Marduk* meaning ruler of the universe.

Lugaldurmah: 'King of the Great Bond' uniting heaven and earth, a holy of holies in the temple of *Enlil* in *Nippur* (see *Duranki* and *Ekur*); also throne, a title of *Marduk*.

Lugallanna: 'King of the power and fulness of the heavens', a title of *Marduk*.

Lugalugga: 'King Death,' (?), a title of *Marduk*.

Ma: Or 'Me', divine rules, gifts and powers; the Ma-dress of Inanna includes the signs and insignia with which she armed herself for the journey to hell. See also *Pala*.

Malah: A title of *Marduk*.

Marduk: 'Sun-child' or 'Son of the Sun', the great god of *Babylon* and hero of 'The Babylonian Creation'; see p. 34.

Marukka: with *Marutukku*, a title of *Marduk* with punning allusions to axe, weapon, child, man and creation.

Marutukku: A title of *Marduk*; see *Marukka*.

Mummu: One of the original existences of the universe along with *Apsu* and *Tiamat*; there are several interpretations of this name, see p. 27. There is another Mummu, a title of *Ea* as a creator-god, and hence, in the 'Hymn of the Fifty Names', a title also of *Marduk*.

Namru: 'Brilliance, purity and magical power', a title of *Marduk*.

Namtillaku: 'The comforter and god of life', a title of *Marduk*.

Nanna: The Sumerian Moon-god, Inanna's father who was worshipped especially at *Ur*.

Nari Lugaldimmerankia: 'The deliverer, the supreme ruler of the universe', a title of *Marduk*.

Nēbiru: *Marduk*'s astral name, a planet, usually Jupiter; the meaning changed but at one time it probably referred to the planet at the moment of the spring equinox when it passes from the old year to the new. It can also mean the whole central band of the heavens and is used as such in the account of *Marduk*'s creation of the heavens in Tablet V; it can also mean a centre, pivot or pole. In the 'Hymn of the Fifty Names' it is *Marduk*'s astral title.

Neti: The chief door-keeper of the underworld.

Ningal: 'The Great Lady', *Inanna*'s mother and the wife of *Nanna*.

Ninshubur: *Inanna*'s chief minister and messenger; he appears recently to have changed sex. (See S. Kramer, 'The Sacred Marriage Rite'.)

Ninsun: The mother of *Dumuzi*, one of the three mourning women, also called *Sirtur*, perhaps a deified ewe.

Nippur: A Sumerian city which, though never a great political centre, was the holy city par excellence. *Enlil* was its particular god; see also *Duranki* and *Ekur*. Nippur is the source of many literary tablets.

Nisan: The month in which the spring equinox falls and the Babylonian New Year; see *Akitu*.

Nudimmud: A title of *Ea* as god of wisdom and moulder of men.

Pala: The robe of sovereignty worn by *Inanna*, one of her *Ma*.

Sag-Kal: A kind of snake.

Shamash: The semitic sun-god, Sumerian *Utu*; also the material sun.

Shara: The god of *Umma*.

Shazu: 'Seeing and proclaiming the heart', a title of *Marduk*.

Sigkurshagga: The temple of *Shara*, tutelary god of *Umma*.

Sin: The Akkadian name for the moon, Sumerian *Nanna*.

Sirsir: A title of *Marduk*.

Sirtur: The mother of *Dumuzi*; see *Ninsun*.

Suhgurim: 'Destroyer of his enemies, who annihilates the wicked', a title of *Marduk*.

Sumer: Southern Mesopotamia, the early inhabitants of which are the Sumerians; 'Sumer and *Akkad*' was the name for the whole of southern and central Mesopotamia.

Tables or Tablets of Destiny: Writings that both comprised and constituted the rule of the whole universe, and whose possession gave absolute power.

Tammuz: The semitic form of *Dumuzi*, the subject of many laments and litanies. In Syria and Palestine Tammuz is 'the Lord' Adonis; in the *Adapa* tale he guards the gate of heaven with *Gizzida*.

Ti'āmat: The primeval waters, one of the eternal existences, but also any stretch of water, sea or lake; see p. 25.

Tuku: 'The mysterious power of words', the binding of a spell; one of the titles of *Marduk*.

Tutu: 'Begetter and reviver of the gods', the composite *tu-tu* has eighteen meanings; the passage of the 'Hymn of the Fifty Names' in which it comes as a title of *Marduk* is full of punning uses which include 'divine power' and 'turning away'.

Ubshukinna: The Chamber of Destinies, a room in the temple complex in *Babylon*, also the great assembly place of the gods in heaven and the scene of much of 'The Babylonian Creation'; see also *Dumuduku* and p. 37.

Umma: A Sumerian city in the south of Mesopotamia.

Ur: An important city in the south of Mesopotamia, the chief city of the moon-god *Nanna*.

Uruk: Biblical Erech, modern Warka, an important city in southern Mesopotamia where the goddess *Inanna* had her chief temple; its early kings used *Dumuzi* as a title and were to some extent identified with the god. Gilgamesh was king of Uruk.

Usmu: The servant of *Marduk*'s mother *Damkina* in 'The Babylonian Creation'.

Utu: The Sumerian sun-god and brother of *Inanna*; like his semitic counterpart *Shamash* he was a just judge and law-giver. In the courtship songs of Inanna it was Utu who urged her to marry *Dumuzi*.

Zabalam: An unidentified Sumerian city.

Zahgurim: 'Destroyer' but also 'the preserver of his companions'; a typically ambiguous title of *Marduk*.

Zahrim: 'Destroyer of the wicked', a title of *Marduk*.

Ziggurat: A stepped pyramid usually built of brick and an essential part of any Mesopotamian temple-complex; the great ziggurat at *Babylon* was called Etemenanki, 'the house of the foundation of heaven and earth'.

Ziku: 'Pure life and breath', a title of *Marduk*.

Zisi: A title of *Marduk*.

Ziukkinna: 'The life of the gods, their leader and ruler', a title of *Marduk*.

Zulum: 'Who cuts the clay', a title of *Marduk*.

FOR THE BEST IN PAPERBACKS, LOOK FOR THE

In every corner of the world, on every subject under the sun, Penguin represents quality and variety – the very best in publishing today.

For complete information about books available from Penguin – including Pelicans, Puffins, Peregrines and Penguin Classics – and how to order them, write to us at the appropriate address below. Please note that for copyright reasons the selection of books varies from country to country.

In the United Kingdom: Please write to *Dept E.P., Penguin Books Ltd, Harmondsworth, Middlesex, UB7 0DA*

In the United States: Please write to *Dept BA, Penguin, 299 Murray Hill Parkway, East Rutherford, New Jersey 07073*

In Canada: Please write to *Penguin Books Canada Ltd, 2801 John Street, Markham, Ontario L3R 1B4*

In Australia: Please write to the *Marketing Department, Penguin Books Australia Ltd, P.O. Box 257, Ringwood, Victoria 3134*

In New Zealand: Please write to the *Marketing Department, Penguin Books (NZ) Ltd, Private Bag, Takapuna, Auckland 9*

In India: Please write to *Penguin Overseas Ltd, 706 Eros Apartments, 56 Nehru Place, New Delhi, 110019*

In Holland: Please write to *Penguin Books Nederland B.V., Postbus 195, NL–1380AD Weesp, Netherlands*

In Germany: Please write to *Penguin Books Ltd, Friedrichstrasse 10–12, D–6000 Frankfurt Main 1, Federal Republic of Germany*

In Spain: Please write to *Longman Penguin España, Calle San Nicolas 15, E–28013 Madrid, Spain*

In France: Please write to *Penguin Books Ltd, 39 Rue de Montmorency, F-75003, Paris, France*

In Japan: Please write to *Longman Penguin Japan Co Ltd, Yamaguchi Building, 2–12–9 Kanda Jimbocho, Chiyoda-Ku, Tokyo 101, Japan*

FOR THE BEST IN PAPERBACKS, LOOK FOR THE

PENGUIN CLASSICS

Netochka Nezvanova Fyodor Dostoyevsky

Dostoyevsky's first book tells the story of 'Nameless Nobody' and introduces many of the themes and issues which will dominate his great masterpieces.

Selections from the Carmina Burana A verse translation by David Parlett

The famous songs from the *Carmina Burana* (made into an oratorio by Carl Orff) tell of lecherous monks and corrupt clerics, drinkers and gamblers, and the fleeting pleasures of youth.

Fear and Trembling Søren Kierkegaard

A profound meditation on the nature of faith and submission to God's will which examines with startling originality the story of Abraham and Isaac.

Selected Prose Charles Lamb

Lamb's famous essays (under the strange pseudonym of Elia) on anything and everything have long been celebrated for their apparently innocent charm; this major new edition allows readers to discover the darker and more interesting aspects of Lamb.

The Picture of Dorian Gray Oscar Wilde

Wilde's superb and macabre novella, one of his supreme works, is reprinted here with a masterly Introduction and valuable Notes by Peter Ackroyd.

A Treatise of Human Nature David Hume

A universally acknowledged masterpiece by 'the greatest of all British Philosophers' – A. J. Ayer

A Passage to India   E. M. Forster

Centred on the unresolved mystery in the Marabar Caves, Forster's great work provides the definitive evocation of the British Raj.

The Republic   Plato

The best-known of Plato's dialogues, *The Republic* is also one of the supreme masterpieces of Western philosophy whose influence cannot be overestimated.

The Life of Johnson   James Boswell

Perhaps the finest 'life' ever written, Boswell's *Johnson* captures for all time one of the most colourful and talented figures in English literary history.

Remembrance of Things Past (3 volumes)   Marcel Proust

This revised version by Terence Kilmartin of C. K. Scott Moncrieff's original translation has been universally acclaimed – available for the first time in paperback.

Metamorphoses   Ovid

A golden treasury of myths and legends which has proved a major influence on Western literature.

A Nietzsche Reader   Friedrich Nietzsche

A superb selection from all the major works of one of the greatest thinkers and writers in world literature, translated into clear, modern English.

Aeschylus	**The Oresteia** **(Agamemnon/Choephori/Eumenides)** **Prometheus Bound/The Suppliants/Seven** **Against Thebes/The Persians**
Aesop	**Fables**
Ammianus Marcellinus	**The Later Roman Empire (A.D. 353–378)**
Apollonius of Rhodes	**The Voyage of Argo**
Apuleius	**The Golden Ass**
Aristophanes	**The Knights/Peace/The Birds/The Assembly** **Women/Wealth**
	Lysistrata/The Acharnians/The Clouds/
	The Wasps/The Poet and the Women/The Frogs
Aristotle	**The Athenian Constitution**
	The Ethics
	The Politics
	De Anima
Arrian	**The Campaigns of Alexander**
Saint Augustine	**City of God**
	Confessions
Boethius	**The Consolation of Philosophy**
Caesar	**The Civil War**
	The Conquest of Gaul
Catullus	**Poems**
Cicero	**The Murder Trials**
	The Nature of the Gods
	On the Good Life
	Selected Letters
	Selected Political Speeches
	Selected Works
Euripides	**Alcestis/Iphigenia in Tauris/Hippolytus/The** **Bacchae/Ion/The Women of Troy/Helen**
	Medea/Hecabe/Electra/Heracles
	Orestes/The Children of Heracles/ **Andromache/The Suppliant Woman/** **The Phoenician Women/Iphigenia in Aulis**

PENGUIN CLASSICS

Hesiod/Theognis	**Theogony** and **Works and Days/Elegies**
'Hippocrates'	**Hippocratic Writings**
Homer	**The Iliad**
	The Odyssey
Horace	**Complete Odes and Epodes**
Horace/Persius	**Satires** and **Epistles**
Juvenal	**Sixteen Satires**
Livy	**The Early History of Rome**
	Rome and Italy
	Rome and the Mediterranean
	The War with Hannibal
Lucretius	**On the Nature of the Universe**
Marcus Aurelius	**Meditations**
Martial	**Epigrams**
Ovid	**The Erotic Poems**
	The Metamorphoses
Pausanias	**Guide to Greece** (in two volumes)
Petronius/Seneca	**The Satyricon/The Apocolocyntosis**
Pindar	**The Odes**
Plato	**Gorgias**
	The Last Days of Socrates (Euthyphro/The Apology/Crito/Phaedo)
	The Laws
	Phaedrus and **Letters VII and VIII**
	Philebus
	Protagoras and **Meno**
	The Republic
	The Symposium
	Timaeus and **Critias**
Plautus	**The Pot of Gold/The Prisoners/The Brothers Menaechmus/The Swaggering Soldier/Pseudolus**
	The Rope/Amphitryo/The Ghost/A Three-Dollar Day

PENGUIN CLASSICS

Pliny	**The Letters of the Younger Pliny**
Plutarch	**The Age of Alexander** (Nine Greek Lives)
	The Fall of the Roman Republic (Six Lives)
	The Makers of Rome (Nine Lives)
	The Rise and Fall of Athens (Nine Greek Lives)
	On Sparta
Polybius	**The Rise of the Roman Empire**
Procopius	**The Secret History**
Propertius	**The Poems**
Quintus Curtius Rufus	**The History of Alexander**
Sallust	**The Jugurthine War** and **The Conspiracy of Cataline**
Seneca	**Four Tragedies** and **Octavia**
	Letters from a Stoic
Sophocles	**Electra/Women of Trachis/Philoctetes/Ajax**
	The Theban Plays (King Oedipus/Oedipus at Colonus/Antigone)
Suetonius	**The Twelve Caesars**
Tacitus	**The Agricola** and **The Germania**
	The Annals of Imperial Rome
	The Histories
Terence	**The Comedies (The Girl from Andros/The Self-Tormentor/The Eunuch/Phormio/The Mother-in-Law/The Brothers)**
Theaetitus	**Early Socratic Diologues (Euthydemus/Hippias Major/Hippias Minor/Lysis/Charmides/Laches/Ion)**
Thucydides	**The History of the Peloponnesian War**
Tibullus	**The Poems** and **The Tibullan Collection**
Virgil	**The Aeneid**
	The Eclogues
	The Georgics
Xenophon	**A History of My Times**
	The Persian Expedition

PENGUIN CLASSICS

Saint Anselm	**The Prayers and Meditations**
Saint Augustine	**The Confessions**
Bede	**A History of the English Church and People**
Chaucer	**The Canterbury Tales**
	Love Visions
	Troilus and Criseyde
Froissart	**The Chronicles**
Geoffrey of Monmouth	**The History of the Kings of Britain**
Gerald of Wales	**History and Topography of Ireland**
	The Journey through Wales and **The Description of Wales**
Gregory of Tours	**The History of the Franks**
Julian of Norwich	**Revelations of Divine Love**
William Langland	**Piers the Ploughman**
Sir John Mandeville	**The Travels of Sir John Mandeville**
Marguerite de Navarre	**The Heptameron**
Christine de Pisan	**The Treasure of the City of Ladies**
Marco Polo	**The Travels**
Richard Rolle	**The Fire of Love**
Thomas à Kempis	**The Imitation of Christ**

ANTHOLOGIES AND ANONYMOUS WORKS

The Age of Bede
Alfred the Great
Beowulf
A Celtic Miscellany
The Cloud of Unknowing and Other Works
The Death of King Arthur
The Earliest English Poems
Early Christian Writings
Early Irish Myths and Sagas
Egil's Saga
The Letters of Abelard and Heloise
Medieval English Verse
Njal's Saga
Seven Viking Romances
Sir Gawain and the Green Knight
The Song of Roland

109143